Reason and Experience

The Representation of Natural Order in the Work of
Carl von Linné

Charles Linné

Reason and Experience

THE REPRESENTATION OF
NATURAL ORDER IN
THE WORK OF CARL VON LINNÉ

by James L. Larson

UNIVERSITY OF CALIFORNIA PRESS
BERKELEY · LOS ANGELES · LONDON

1971

UNIVERSITY OF CALIFORNIA PRESS

BERKELEY AND LOS ANGELES

UNIVERSITY OF CALIFORNIA PRESS, LTD.

LONDON, ENGLAND

ISBN: 0-520-01834-6

LIBRARY OF CONGRESS CATALOG CARD NO.: 70-632164

COPYRIGHT © 1971 BY THE REGENTS OF THE UNIVERSITY OF CALIFORNIA

DESIGNED BY DAVE COMSTOCK

Contents

Preface

I am attempting here to solve one of the oldest problems in Linnæan scholarship—the nature and extent of the subterranean connection between logical forms and natural forms implicit in Linné's system of nature. I have approached the problem through the speculative, experimental, professional, and religious terms in which system and method presented themselves to Linné; by analyzing the role of these terms in the creation of the Linnæan systematic structure, this study indicates some of that structure's chief presuppositions and principles.

The difficulties in penetrating the material for this study could not have been overcome without the conceptual framework and many of the insights afforded by the earlier inquiries of Henri Daudin and Ernst Cassirer. These scholars have been given what must appear rather short shrift in my work, but I do not want this book to appear without an expression of my indebtedness.

Chapters II and IV were printed in an earlier form in *Isis*, Vol. 58 and Vol. 59, and I thank Dr. Robert P. Multhauf for permission to use them here.

I also wish to thank the University of California for a Traveling Fellowship in 1963–1964, and a Summer Faculty Grant in 1969.

Finally, I wish to express my gratitude to the faculties of the German Department, University of Pennsylvania, and of Comparative Literature and Scandinavian, University of California, Berkeley, for their acceptance and encouragement of work which lies so far outside their commitments and sympathies.

Introduction

A study of Carl von Linné's system of classification is by no means a novelty. In his own century it was examined critically by Buffon, Kant, and Goethe; lesser figures continued the discussion, and by the end of the eighteenth century the Linnæan system was an established topic in natural history.

Since then it has been investigated in more or less detail by Cuvier, Lamarck, Saint-Hilaire, A.-P. de Candolle, and Darwin. The special contribution of the twentieth century has been the scholarly rediscovery of Linné. After Ewald Ährling's edition of the *Ungdomsskrifter* came the editions of the *Vetenskapsakademi*, of the *Linné-Sällskap*, of Arvid Hjalmar Uggla, of Elis Malmeström, and of others, the bibliographies of Hulth and Soulsby, the republication of the Linnæan travels, and the facsimile editions of W. T. Stearn. The secondary literature relating to the Linnæan system is now so large it frustrates inquiry. The thought of no other naturalist–save perhaps Aristotle or Darwin–has received more attention.

For the purposes of my study discussion of the Linnæan system has been divided into two kinds–that of philosophers and that of scientists. There is, of course, no fixed boundary between philosophic and scientific discourse, but there does seem to be a different approach to inquiry. Confronted with one of the concepts of the Linnæan system, for example, a philosopher moves to the underlying problem of abstraction, and then to the metaphysical presuppositions implied; a scientist, on the other hand, moves from the general problem to particular examples which exemplify or disallow general statements. That is to say, a philosopher interests himself in the elements of order which imply a stance toward all reality, while a scientist serializes his problems so as to find a particular solution for each of them. The difficulties raised by these two approaches are more apparent when they are considered in detail.

In a chapter on "The Problem of Classifying and Systematizing Natural Forms" in the fourth volume of *The Problem of Knowledge*, Ernst Cassirer has dealt with the question of classifying natural objects in the eighteenth century. His essay discusses the Linnæan system in some detail from a philosopher's point of view. Cassirer first points out the inner bond between Aristotelian class logic and the Linnæan system, and then raises the questions discussed by Kant in the first introduction to the *Critique of Judgment*: What justifies the naturalist in seeing nature as a whole which assumes the form of a natural system? Whence comes the harmony between natural forms and logical forms? This, says Cassirer, is the problem contained in Linné's work, and Kant, in showing that a system is a query addressed to nature to which only experience can give an adequate answer, speaks as the logician of Linnæan science. With this sleight of hand Cassirer eliminates dogmatic assertions of a preestablished harmony between natural and logical forms.

He then asks whether the Linnæan method of comparing natural objects and grouping them according to formal similarities moves in the realm of things, or in the realm of mere names. The answer to this question has already been decided, for concepts based upon formal comparison are empty unless one assumes that such comparisons attain the fundamental relations in reality. Directly the harmony between nature and the understanding is questioned, the assumption becomes tenuous. Using Linné's binary nomenclature and the so-called "artificial" method of classification to stand for the whole of Linnæan descriptive practice, Cassirer concludes that Linné's system never moves beyond the problems of mere recognition and identification of natural objects. The flaw in this approach is that Cassirer requires an analogy drawn between class logic and the Linnæan system to hold in everything; he would not have the operations of the system occasionally to resemble, but to be, an Aristotelian class logic. This enables Cassirer to uncover the metaphysical presuppositions of the Linnæan system

with great perspicuity, and at the same time to do a great injustice
to Linné's descriptive science.[1]

The danger of the opposite approach, generalization from
particulars, is seen in H. K. Svenson's paper "On the Descriptive
Method of Linnæus." Svenson shows that entries in the *Species
plantarum*, especially in American and Asian flora, which for Linné
represent nonessential variations, are, in fact, distinct species. The
entries under the American oaks, for example, consist of two or
more species by present standards. On the basis of this evidence
Svenson concludes that Linnæan species in general are more inclu-
sive than the species of today.[2] Upon consideration of the nature
of Linné's herbarium and other evidence, Svenson might have
concluded more justifiably that Linné's aggregate species issue from
bad or insufficient material rather than a broad species concept.[3]

In short, though the scientific and philosophic approach to
inquiry differ, both have been guilty of the same error of principle,
for they have assumed repeatedly that the considerations which
govern Linné's work are wholly speculative or wholly empirical.
The tasks of the eighteenth-century naturalist utilized, as Buffon
pointed out long ago, sweeping speculative views and painstakingly
minute observation. A full consideration of eighteenth-century natural history might consider as well the scientific importance of
other traits prominent in the work of the period—scholastic erudition, for example, and artistic sensitivity. But for purposes of my
study, the point has been made: Linnæan scholarship has been
content for too long a time to stress the role of a single set of
considerations in Linné's systematic work.

I am attempting to restore some of the complexity of Linné's
descriptive enterprise through an inquiry into the terms in which
the problem of a "natural method" presented itself to Linné. In

1. Ernst Cassirer, *The Problem of Knowledge. Philosophy, Science, and History Since
   Hegel* (1950), pp. 118–136.
2. H. K. Svenson, "On the Descriptive Method of Linnæus," *Rhodora* 47 (1945):
   273–302, 363–388.
3. See W. T. Stearn, "An Introduction to the *Species Plantarum* and cognate
   botanical works of Carl Linnæus," *Species Plantarum, a Facsimile of the
   first edition, 1753,* vol. 1 (1957), pp. 159–160.

explaining his own work Linné tried to derive all scientific knowledge from reason and experience. Reason, he asserts, suggests notions either anticipatory to or interpretive of fact, and then, once experience has furnished the matter of knowledge, weighs findings, draws conclusions, discovers truth, and decides questions.[4]

These exemplary but vague terms, reason and experience, do not, however, account for the entire structure of Linné's systematic thought; they interact with professional exigencies, scientific traditions, and religious beliefs. In establishing the role played in the creation of Linné's system by all of these considerations, and by showing how they gravitate toward one central topic—the discovery of the intelligible as it is manifest in things felt and seen—I have attempted to describe a body of practice and a resultant systematic structure which both limited and advanced scientific description.

The character of my study, which is concerned less with results than with the formative forces in Linné's system, has imposed some limitations on the discussion. Perhaps regrettably, the discussion is limited to botany, the first and last work of Linné, and his favorite study. As Daudin pointed out, Linné's theory with respect to the animal kingdom remained constant, but the facts upon which Linné based his theory differ.[5] The concessions and qualifications which these further considerations involve would add to the extent but not to the clarity of this study.

Moreover, this is a discussion of the conception of natural order as it was understood in eighteenth-century natural history—a hierarchy of concepts and definitions which, in expressing the essential similarities of objects, sought to represent the system of nature. Understood in this way, my study has very little to do with modern systematics or logic. Rather, it is an investigation of that tradition of "empty verbiage and barren scholasticism" (as

<hr>

4. "Oratio, qua peregrinationum intra patriam asseritur necessitas," *Amoenitates academicæ*, vol. 2 (1787), pp. 409–410. All subsequent reference to the *Amoenitates academicæ* is to this edition (1785–1789), cited hereafter *A.A.*

5. Henri Daudin, *De Linné à Jussieu, Méthodes de la Classification et idée de série en botanique et en zoologie (1740–1790)* (1926), pp. 76–77. For a somewhat different view see Nils von Hofsten, "Systema naturæ, ett tvåhundraårsminne," *Svenska-Linné-Sällskapets Årsskrift,* Årg. XVIII (1935), pp. 1–15. See especially pp. 8–9.

Sir Karl Popper describes it[6]), which is the Aristotelian method. This is only to assert, although somewhat emphatically, that the presuppositions and principles of science differ markedly from one age to another and entail very different approaches to the representation of natural order.

The conduct of the discussion may be summarized thus: Chapter I touches upon the history of the problem of order which confronted eighteenth-century natural history. The analysis of this problem reveals a conflict in the practical and theoretical tendencies in the work of the preceding period. The remainder of the study is devoted to an analysis of the conflict of these tendencies in the work of Carl von Linné. Chapters II to IV analyze in terms of practical needs and observed affinities a systematic structure composed of five strata, each stratum with peculiar problems, all strata interacting with one another. Each chapter follows a similar course, beginning with theoretical concepts, proceeding to practical constitution, and concluding with formal definition. Chapter V is concerned with nomenclature and the satisfaction of practical and theoretical requirements. The Conclusion draws together various problems raised in the four preceding chapters, and shows how the considerations which lie behind these problems involve the more profound assumptions of eighteenth-century natural history concerning the system, the elements, and the representation of order.

6. Karl R. Popper, *The Open Society and Its Enemies* (1950), p. 206.

Chapter I

THE SYSTEM OF NATURE
AND THE NATURAL METHOD

Conditions favoring development of and reflection upon the procedures of classification were first realized in modern natural history in the plant kingdom, and for more than two centuries the study of plant forms remained slightly in advance of the study of the more complex and less easily observed forms in the animal kingdom.[1]

To trace the origin of modern systematics to the herbalists is nowadays something of a heresy. Since the appearance of Julius von Sachs' classic *History of Botany,* it has been customary to stress the herbalists' immediate intuitive connection with nature, and to deemphasize one of the strongest tendencies in their work, the tendency toward an integrated system. Sachs' rather narrow ideas about scientific method led him to stress the elements of objective science in the herbals and to overlook transgressions of the limits of observation. On the basis of his interpretation Sachs then proposed two contrasting methods in sixteenth-century natural history. The herbalists, led by sound scientific instinct, established only such loosely defined groupings of plant forms as presented themselves to the unprejudiced eye; Cæsalpino and his followers, on the other hand, influenced by a pernicious logical method, insti-

1. Henri Daudin, *De Linné à Jussieu, Méthodes de la Classification et idée de série en botanique et en zoologie (1740–1790)* (1926), pp. 21–22; Rud. Burckhardt, "J.-V. Carus, Geschichte der Zoologie, 1872," *Zoologische Annalen,* (1905): 369–371.

tuted sharply differentiated groupings of plant forms on the basis of preconceived principles.[2]

This rationale has never proven wholly adequate to the historical understanding of this early period. The two contrasting methods proposed by Sachs did, after all, share a single aim, the elaboration of the system of nature in the plant kingdom, and the methods used to achieve this aim were not completely antagonistic. Both approaches utilized, as recent research has established, intuitive total impressions in constituting plant groups; both approaches distinguished more or less clearly circumstantial accidents from essential features in defining these groups; both approaches eventually made extensive use of Aristotelian theory and practice; and the results of both approaches implied the actual existence of a class hierarchy as one of the most obvious elements of natural order. Sachs' proposal of two antagonistic methods has obscured these bonds of continuity in aims, materials, methods, and achievements.

Any attempt to understand the herbalists' contribution to the classification of natural form may well begin with their gradual emancipation from classical authority. (For some useful information on this topic, see Jerry Stannard, "The Graeco-Roman Background of the Renaissance Herbal," *Organon* 4 (1967: 141–145 and idem, "The Herbal as a Medical Document," *Bulletin Historical Medicine* 43 (1969): 212–220.) This emancipation was, of course, never complete; in matters of nomenclature and the broad divisions of plant forms Theophrastus, Dioscorides, Galen, and Pliny exerted a powerful influence. The herbals contain extensive notes on Greek and Latin nomenclature, and nearly all adopt some version of the general division of the plant kingdom of Theophrastus or Dioscorides. A central concern of the herbalists, however, was the practical identification of individual plant forms. On this point the moderns very quickly discovered the fallibility of the ancients, whose plant descriptions, even when reviewed and corrected by the commentators of the fifteenth century, were often vague and incomplete.

---

2. Julius von Sachs, *History of Botany* (1530–1860) (1890), pp. 4–7, 23–26, etc. The interpretation has been retained by Em. Rádl, *Geschichte der Biologischen Theorien seit dem Ende des siebzehnten Jahrhunderts*, I. Teil (1905); and Walter Zimmermann, *Evolution, die Geschichte ihrer Probleme und Erkenntnisse* (1935).

The herbalists also found rather quickly that the plants of Dioscorides do not grow everywhere in Europe, and conversely, many European plants are not listed by Dioscorides. The discovery led to an accumulation of descriptions of individual plants, and, almost simultaneously, to groupings of these forms on the basis of general outward appearance.

The instinctive impulse, says Hélène Metzger,

> when we come upon things unknown to us, consists in comparing them to things we believe we already know, in finding among them resemblances and differences; in short, in placing what we have just come upon in the imperfect picture of the world to which we are habituated, and which we aspire to complete.[3]

This elementary reaction establishes groupings based upon a single common quality—cut, color, use, etc.—or upon a manifold of unanalyzed qualities grasped immediately; established spontaneously, the groupings tend to collapse with equal rapidity. If, however, we consider the intellectual reaction rather than the unstable and inconsistent results, we discover many of the germs of later conceptualization. The herbals of the German fathers of botany provide one example of these elementary processes of conceptualization.

These processes, even in their simplest form—Otto Brunfels' *Herbarum vivæ eicones*[4]—cannot be reduced to the mere accumulation of particular plants. This beautiful old herbal, half encyclopædia, half provincial flora, is illustrated with the woodcuts of Hans Weyditz. There are matching notes on classical and German nomenclature, descriptions of temperament, locale, time, virtues, sententiæ extracted from Theophrastus, Dioscorides, Galen, and Pliny, and a list of authors who have described the plant previously. Although the descriptions are tentative and vague, and correlated only with the most general outward aspects of form, Brunfels has grasped the idea of a type: his work attempts to coordinate a body of information and a single name with all those plant forms which are sufficiently similar that their particular differences can be overlooked without inconvenience. Brunfels' attempts to bring together larger groups of these forms under a single designation

3. Hélène Metzger, *Les Concepts Scientifiques* (1926), p. 15.
4. Otto Brunfels, *Herbarvm vivæ eicones* (1530).

are not far advanced. He uses very occasionally the words *genera* and *typi*; they seem never to implicate more than two or three plant forms. The texts and woodcuts throughout the volume do not seem to be arranged according to any general systematic principle.

The sense of formal resemblances grows more explicit in the herbals of Hieronymus Bock, Valerius Cordus, and Leonhart Fuchs. The groupings of plant forms implied in the format of these herbals are so pronounced, that both Sachs and Daudin have argued that systematics originates, not in the consideration of individual kinds, but in the perception of larger groups. Affinities are inferred, not from the close comparison of parts, but from gross likenesses often more obvious than individual differences.

> In undertaking to describe individual forms, the first task
> was to separate those which closely resembled one another,
> for the resemblance of systematically-allied plants is often
> so great, that to distinguish them specifically requires consid-
> eration and careful comparison.[5]

In some such way, the attempt to arrive at and fix individual forms may have led directly to the conception of a distinctly systematic arrangement.

Bock has discussed some of these problems in the fourteenth chapter of the *Vorrede* to the *Kreüter Buch*. He declares himself against alphabetical order, which separates like and juxtaposes unlike plant forms, proposing in its place a tripartite division based upon but diverging quaintly from that of Theophrastus: first, all common wild and tame plants and roots; next, clover plants *(Klee Kreüttern)*; and finally, all German bushes, hedges, thorns, fruitful and unfruitful trees, tame as well as wild. Within this general division Bock holds to process and order, setting like with like, and separating unlike from unlike. These subordinate groupings, carried out in the herbal, rest upon little more than general outward appearance. A good example, pointed out by Sachs, is Bock's placement of the wind bell *(Convolvulus)* in the midst of other climbing, twining, and trailing plants.[6]

5. Sachs, pp. 23–24. Henri Daudin, *Cuvier et Lamarck, les Classes Zoologiques et l'idée de série animale (1790–1830)* (1926), vol. 1, pp. 3–4.
6. Hieronymus Bock, *Kreüter Buch* (1560); Sachs, pp. 27–28.

The systematic bifurcation utilized by Bock was to last until the time of Linné. The most general division of plant forms, here taken from Theophrastus (but occasionally taken from Dioscorides), imposes an abstract framework, dividing plants into easily manageable, approximately equal sections. Within this framework smaller groups are established on the basis of an unanalyzed total impression, then worked out in more or less detail and rather carefully rationalized.

This same bifurcation can be found in Valerius Cordus' *Historiæ Stirpium Lib. IIII Posthumi.*[7] As the title indicates the work is divided in four parts, again reflecting the influence of Theophrastus' general division of plants. Within this framework, however, the term "genus" is used as a class concept to organize subordinate species descriptions. Cordus' treatment of the *Ranunculi* offers a good example. He lists twelve species, first *Ranunculus palustris*, then *Secunda species, Tertia species, Quarta species*, etc. The *Ranunculus palustris*, the first or chief species of the genus, is given very full treatment. Cordus notes locale, form (stems, branches, leaves, flowers, seeds, and roots), and virtues. The other species of the genus he compares with this full description, and only those aspects in which they differ from the first species are noted.[8]

Leonhart Fuchs' *De Historia stirpium*[9] establishes a separate terminology of one hundred and thirty plant elements, ranging from *Acetabula* to *Vngues*, an indication, as Sachs points out, of the increasing importance of the analysis of parts.[10] Fuchs' use of nomenclature reveals a conscious attempt to group plant forms. He uses a single name for a plant when he does not know forms neighboring the one he describes, as in *Anethum, Aparina, Asclepias,* and *Asparagus*, or when, under the spell of classical authority, he does not draw a relation between two or three species with which he is in fact acquainted, as in *Personatia* and *Xanthium* (both being *Xanthium*), and as in *Coronopus* and *Plantago* (both being *Plantago*). Fuchs' nomenclature becomes binomial, trinomial, or a phrase, when a real or imaginary relation unites two, three, or more plants,

<hr>

7. Valerius Cordus, *Historiæ Stirpium Lib. IIII Posthumi* (1541).
8. Ibid., pp. 119–121. See also R. Dughi, "Tournefort dans l'histoire de la botanique," *Tournefort* (1957), p. 140.
9. *De Historia Stirpium* (1546).
10. Sachs, pp. 20–21.

as in *Elleborus albus, Elleborus niger sylvestris, Elleborus niger adulterinus hortensis*,[11] and in *Nymphæa candida, Nymphæa lutea*,[12] and in *Chelidonium maius, Chelidonium minus*.[13] The designation of two plants with one name does not always indicate a real relationship. Today *Viola purpurea* is regarded as a violet, while *Viola matronalis* and *Viola matronalis punicea* are placed among the *Cruciferæ*.[14]

In short, the herbals of the German fathers of botany unfold the elementary processes of formal conceptualization step by step. The earliest descriptions are oriented, not toward a particular form, but toward a type, and the type, very often, can be established only when correlated with other nearly related types. As the herbalist fixes individual plant forms through woodcuts, written descriptions, and investigations into nomenclature, he groups these forms on the basis of resemblances at first vaguely indicated, if at all. The resemblances are then objectified linguistically with a common name for two or more forms, and this identification leads to a more profound analysis of the likenesses, as well as of the specific differences, manifested by each form so designated.

These same elementary processes, from the relative stabilization of individual forms to the explicitation of general resemblances, are found in the works of the *trois grands Hollandais* of a slightly later period, Charles de l'Écluse, Rembert Dodoens, and Matthias de l'Obel.

L'Écluse, in the *Rariorum Plantarum Historia*,[15] retains two characteristic features from the German herbals, the investigation of plants known to the ancients, and the description of individual forms. These were activities perfectly adapted to l'Écluse's own gifts, for in these matters he was to Dodoens, says Tournefort, as a master to a child.[16] In ordering plants, however, l'Écluse became Dodoens' dependent. His smaller groups, implicit in the order of the herbal, parallel the arrangements of Dodoens and l'Obel,

11. Fuchs, p. 96.
12. Fuchs, pp. 185–186.
13. Fuchs, pp. 292–294.
14. Fuchs, p. 108.
15. Charles de l'Écluse, *Rariorvm Plantarum Historia* (1601).
16. Josef Pitton de Tournefort, "Isagoge in Rem Herbariam," in *Tournefort* (1957), p. 276.

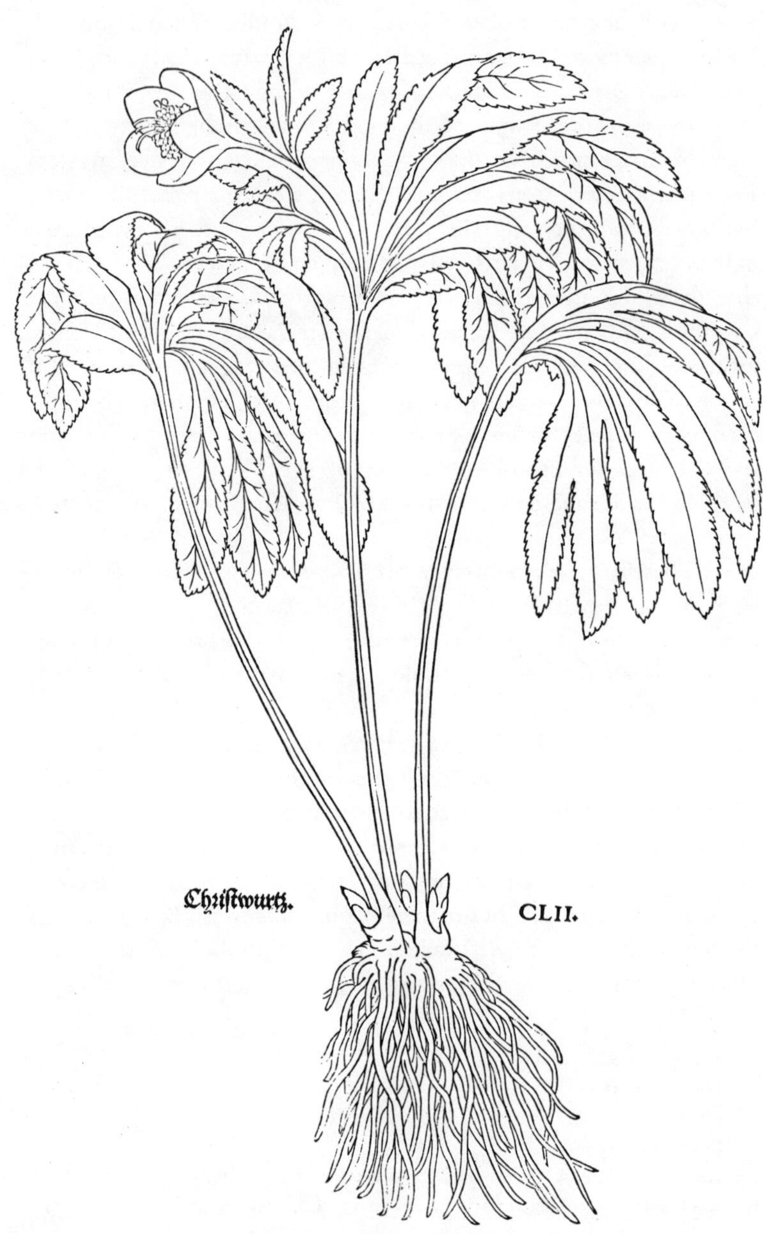

Chelidonium maius or *Christwurtz* from Fuchs' *De Historia Stirpium.*

and his attempt to situate plants in a development from the less to the more perfect parallels l'Obel.[17]

The contrast between the work of l'Écluse and that of Dodoens and l'Obel should not, however, be overstressed. The work of the three herbalists is more in the nature of an extended collaboration. The same elements appear in the work of all, weighted by each somewhat differently. Dodoens' and l'Obel's works also investigate plants known to the ancients, and describe individual forms according to their "kyndes and differences." The focus shifts, however, in Dodoens imperceptibly, in l'Obel markedly, from the individual types to the problems of grouping by art and affinity.

In the foreword to the *Pemptades* Dodoens sanctions the systematic bifurcation already touched upon in relation to Bock's *Kreüter Bůch*.[18] Dodoens recognizes that the larger divisions of the plant kingdom are not imposed by any observed resemblance, and that they are not to be considered *genera majora et minora*; these divisions have a purely practical purpose, that of parceling out the plant kingdom. In the *Pemptades* itself Dodoens subdivides each of the six Pemptads into five books arranged alphabetically. Within this framework, however, Dodoens worked out many small groups on the basis of outward appearance, and juxtaposed these groups with related forms, revealing, as Meyer pointed out long ago, a knowledge of many of the larger genera and families, as well as many not at all obvious plant relations.[19] Umbelliferous plants, for example, are treated as a distinct group in a chapter, *De Umbelliferis Herbis*.

These intuitive groupings are carried even further in the *Nova Stirpium Adversaria* of Pierre Pena and Matthias de l'Obel.[20] In the execution of this work, considered by some older commentators as the first rude sketch of a natural method of arrangement,[21]

17. See Sachs, pp. 29–32. The idea of arranging natural forms in a graded *scala naturæ* according to their order of perfection is, of course, Aristotelian. See A. O. Lovejoy, *The Great Chain of Being* (1936), pp. 58–59.

18. Rembert Dodoens, *Stirpium historiæ pemptades sex sive libri XXX* (1583), pp. 1–4. See also p. 21.

19. Ernst H. F. Meyer, *Geschichte der Botanik* (1856) 3. Band, pp. 348–349.

20. Matthias l'Obel and Pierre Pena, *Nova Stirpium Adversaria Perfacilis Vestigatio* (1576).

21. See, for example, Richard Pulteney, *Historical and Biographical Sketches of the Progress of Botany in England from its Origin to the Introduction of the Linnæan System* (1790), p. 101.

l'Obel tried to make his arrangements explicit. At the head of each of his forty-four major groups he gave a synopsis of all the species to be described based upon general outward appearance. The major groups, as Vines indicates, contain plants of one, two, or more modern genera, and some, it must be confessed, very incongruous to each other.[22]

The classifications of the herbalists of the Netherlands and Germany have only a limited merit; the herbals did, however, accomplish three important tasks: they freed plant study from the exclusive authority of the ancients; they increased the number of known plants; and they carried out a preliminary division of plant groups on the basis of general outward appearance. On this latter point, whether by accident or design, the practices of the herbalists agreed with certain procedures set forth by Aristotle for constituting a natural system. Almost all of the herbalists attempted, for example, largely following the indications afforded by common appellation, to constitute small, closely allied groups of plant forms. They treated the common attributes of such groups generically, and divided them from groups with differing attributes. The apparently tentative, haphazard process of using outward likenesses for group differentiae was, in reality, a step toward the differentiation of forms according to the next higher genus and specific differences.

22. Sydney Howard Vines, "Robert Morison and John Ray," *Makers of British Botany* (1913), p. 10. See also Sachs' treatment, pp. 31–32. As an example of l'Obel's synopses, *Graminis omne Genus*

		Maius
	Vulgatis pratense	Minus
		Minimum
		Rabinum vel Ranisum Montanum
		foliis vetonicæ Caryophyllatæ

Gramen

| Caninum | longius radicatum | Officinarum |
| | Bulbosum nodosum | |

Harundinaceum scabrum, equinex Babylonium aut Cilicium
Harundinaceum læve, & pilosum nemorum schæmum, fortè Pliny
Harundinaceum striatum album
Harundinaceum Marinum
Schæmon vulgare
Parnasi hederaceo, aut Chelidony folio, &
Pliny Aizoi effigie gramina suis locis
Manna esculentum

The Aristotelian element enters quite explicitly into the works of the Swiss herbalists, Konrad Gesner, and Jean and Gaspard Bauhin. Gesner's influence on herbalism was slight, since his compendium of plants, intended to equal his monumental *Historia animalium*, was only published in the eighteenth century and was by then very much out of date.[23] Gesner remains, however, a central figure in any study of sixteenth-century systematics: he had conceived a classification by genus and species as early as 1559;[24] he transferred the Aristotelian principle of continuity to herbalism from zoology; he seems to have conceived and executed a comparative organography; and finally, he was one of the first to seek the basis of plant classification in fruit and flower. In all of this the influence of Aristotle's systematic thought is readily detected and traced to Gesner's zoological work.

While carrying out the *Historia animalium* Gesner seems to have noted the applicability of Aristotle's systematic principles to the plant kingdom. As Cæsalpino was to do a generation later, Gesner began with the Aristotelian principle of vital unity, and concluded the superiority of fructification over vegetation as a basis for division. In the letter quoted by Tournefort and Adanson, he proposes fruit and flowers in contrast to foliation as his *fundamentum divisionis*.

> It is rather according to these two organs rather than according to the leaves, that the natures and relations of plants appear. It is by these marks that we grasp readily that the *Staphisagria* and the *Consolida* are plants of the same tribe as *Aconitum*.[25]

He admitted that division might be made on the basis of many likenesses, relating plants in a more or less continuous way, all the while distinguishing between essential and accidental marks.

> The *Melissa* of Constantinople appears to relate in some fashion to the *Lamium* or the *Urtica mortuam*, but differing from it in the form of the grain, which customarily serves me in establishing the relations of species.[26]

23. For bibliographical detail see Ernst H. F. Meyer, pp. 330–332.
24. Dughi, p. 140.
25. Tournefort, *Elemens de Botanique ou Méthode pour connoître les Plantes* (1694), p. 17.
26. Ibid., p. 17.

From this and other remarks quoted by Meyer[27] it is clear that Gesner instituted genus and species when they imposed themselves naturally, and that he distinguished between species and varieties on the basis of relative constancy. Gesner seems to have carried out a comparative organography as well. Tournefort quotes Conring to the effect that Gesner

> caused to be drawn and engraved figures according to a singular and otherwise unused method, by dividing the plants in parts and making seen each element separately.[28]

These insights, buried in Gesner's posthumous *Epistolarum medicinalium* and unpublished collections, remained without effect until the second half of the seventeenth century. Among contemporaries and immediate successors Gesner's most influential work on plants was his *Tabulæ de stirpium collectione*.[29]

By general agreement the art of the herbalists culminated in the *Pinax* of Gaspard Bauhin. Inspired by the compilations of his brother Jean, Gaspard conceived his project of a summa of botanical knowledge. Like his brother, he did not live to complete the project, but he managed to publish three preliminary volumes, the *Phytopinax*,[30] the *Prodromos*,[31] and the *Pinax*.[32]

For at least the next century the *Pinax* remained the authoritative concordance of plant names and forms. Since the time of Dioscorides and Pliny, the same plant forms had received many names; since the fifteenth century herbalists had incorrectly applied many old names to regional plants confused with plants described in classical authors. Bauhin spent forty years sorting names and forms; his work was so thoroughly done the *Pinax* became an indispensable guide to the history of the species. Tournefort has described how the *Pinax* was used. Showing first how a novice in plant study may attain the genus of a plant, Tournefort then uses the *Pinax* to arrive at the species.

27. Ernst H. F. Meyer, pp. 333–334.
28. Tournefort, "Isagoge," p. 286.
29. For bibliographical detail see Ernst H. F. Meyer, p. 329.
30. Gaspard Bauhin, φυτοπιναξ (1596).
31. Gaspard Bauhin, προδρόμοs (1671).
32. Gaspard Bauhin, πινάξ (1671).

This done, we must seek the species . . . in the *Pinax* of Gaspard Bauhin, which is an excellent book where this learned man has gathered together all the different names that the authors who preceded him have given to the species of plants. We should examine these species in the authors cited, and if the root, the stem, and all the modifications of their parts answer to the individual description which the authors cited have made of it, we may be assured that the plant we seek to know is a true species . . . for which the name, the description, and the figure are founded in just those authors cited. If these authors have not spoken of the species we seek, we should consult those who have written after Gaspard Bauhin. Finally, if we do not find it in these latter authors, we give it a suitable name; that is to say, we place it under the species . . . by establishing its difference on what we find most singular in this species.[33]

It is clear from this excerpt that a great part of Bauhin's success lies in his systematization. The *Nymphæa*, as Dughi points out, offer a relatively concise example of Bauhin's system. Under the single name *Nymphæa*, Bauhin places two genera, *Nymphæa alba* and *Nymphæa lutea*, each with four subordinate species. The genus *Nymphæa alba*, for example, includes the species *Nymphæa alba major* (followed by its synonyms), *Nymphæa alba minor* (followed by its synonyms), *Nymphæa alba minima* (followed by its synonyms), and *Galum radix aquatica* (which has no synonyms). A simple name such as *Nymphæa* designates a group hierarchically superior to the genera. Under these simple names there is an indication of the classical sources and the genera originally distinguished.[34] Generic names, as in the case of *Nymphæa alba* and *Nymphæa luteo*, usually consist of two or more words, as *Orchis Palmata et Satyrion, Hedera Terrestris,* or *Viola Matronalis Sive Hesperis.* The title of a series of species is often given as *Nymphæa ejusque species, Linum ejusque species, Nigella seu Melanthium ejusque*

33. Tournefort, *Elemens de Botanique*, p. iv.
34. *Pinax*, pp. 193–194. Νυμφαία Theophrasto 9. hist. 13. Dioscoridi I. 3. c. 148. cui sic dicta, quoniam aquosa amet. At Plinio I. 24. c. 7. natam tradit ex Nymphæ Zelotypia erga Herculem, unde quibusdam Heracleon dicatur. Officinis Nenuphar. Genera duo Dioscoridi et Plinio: altera flore albo, radice nigra: altera flore luteo, radice alba.

species. The specific name includes the generic name plus a difference, usually drawn from the morphology, as in *Nymphæa lutea major, Nymphæa lutea minor magno*, etc., but also occasionally from its medicinal uses, as in *Solanum officinarum.*

The *Pinax*, then, establishes differentiae for species previously placed under one name, and simultaneously groups species more rigorously on the basis of general outward appearance. The *Pinax* distinguishes both between species and genus, and between genus and the next higher group. It does not, however, as Sachs claimed, originate binary nomenclature. Bauhin's need for phrase names at the species level shows that he did not, perhaps could not, distinguish between names and definitions, probably because he did not define his genera rigorously. This lack of clearly defined taxa, as Dughi points out, stems from the intuitive methods of herbalism.[35] Bauhin interested himself more in evoking general appearance than in minute morphological detail, and his studies were directed toward groupings established by his predecessors rather than toward new arrangements. As for Bauhin's more general arrangements, the larger groups, as in Gesner's theories, follow one another in such a way, that natural families, when distinguishable, have no sharp limits; the overall pattern, as in l'Obel, proceeds from the less perfect or simpler forms to the more perfect or complex forms. These arrangements are, so to speak, typographical, an effort, as Dughi remarks, *à bout de souffle.*[36]

By the end of the sixteenth century herbalism constituted a science which dealt with a distinct subject in a unique way. The whole system of identifications, differentiations, comparisons, and coordinations grew out of an attempt to relate plant forms on the basis of external resemblances and differences. In the earlier herbals an effort was made to fix under a single name, either in woodcuts or in written descriptions, the typical outer figure of an individual plant form. In Brunfels these forms, when brought together between the covers of a book, were so many *disjecta membra*: it is as if the power of articulation had been exhausted in the number of individual forms. But already in Bock's *Kreüter Bůch* there was an attempt to group forms on the basis of resem-

35. Dughi, p. 147; Sachs, p. 33.
36. Dughi, p. 147.

blances which cannot be made explicit. Forms were not subordinated to a superior concept, but grouped around characteristic features of general outward appearance. In Fuchs this general similarity crystallized in family names, and the first generic concepts, those of Cordus, solved the problems of comparison and differentiation through the use of a first or chief species. Increasingly explicit and comprehensive groupings are found in the works of l'Écluse, Dodoens, and l'Obel. Finally, Bauhin's *Pinax* classed almost 6,000 plant forms according to genus and species, indicating superior groups as well.

It is, as Sachs says, an indication of the intuitive nature of herbalism, that the smaller groups were worked out first.[37] The imperfect state of comparative morphology and the consequent absence of any regular terminology tended to segregate each plant group above the generic level. Plant families, although clearly indicated, were each separate sets of problems; they neither determined one another, nor formed a unitary system. The most general divisions of the plant kingdom were imposed from without, and were used for the purely practical purpose of dividing the kingdom into separate but equal parts.

Sachs interpreted this failure to achieve a rigorously integrated and homogeneous system as a triumph of objective science. Faithful to an immediate and artless connection with nature, the herbalists did not, in their rage for order, transgress the limits of nature, or apply a priori rules of classification to plant forms. A history which approaches the conceptual elements of the herbalists in this way can only regard the differences between the systems of the herbalists and the Aristotelians as a veritable chasm. "These two elements of systematic investigation," says Sachs,

> were entirely incommensurable; it was not possible by the use of arbitrary principles of classification which satisfied the understanding to do justice at the same time to the instinctive feeling for natural affinity which would not be argued away. This incommensurability between natural affinity and *a priori* grounds of classification is everywhere expressed in the systems embracing the whole vegetable kingdom, which were proposed up to 1736, and which, including

37. Sachs, p. 25.

those of Cæsalpino and Linnæus, were not less in number than fifteen.[38]

The formulation is striking, but a different systematic conclusion is inherent in it from the one which Sachs drew. Even when we admit that a transformation was effected in the progress from the herbalists' intuitive groupings to the predetermined principles of Cæsalpino, it is still possible to view that transformation as an evolution.

The process of grouping plant forms on the basis of external likenesses utilizes the same basic conceptual elements found in Aristotelian systems. These elements are three in number: types, differentiae, and an integrating structure. The basic units of order are fixed types of natural forms. These types, constituted from and defined by diverse but limited visual and tactile qualities, or differentiae, are integrated in a structure conceived as an ascending sequence of forms. In the methods of both the herbalists and the Aristotelians, the appearance of these conceptual elements can be traced to the same two presuppositions: the process of comparing and grouping natural forms on the basis of like or comparable parts isolates an essential or determining pattern active in a manifold of individuals; and the grouping process, when used to organize more general classes, establishes a class hierarchy which reproduces the order of nature. It is this common conceptual basis which makes it possible to compare the systematic work of the herbalists and the Aristotelians. The process of classification which begins with the herbalists points more and more precisely, as their procedures grow self-conscious and critical, toward that rigorous determination of class concepts in an integrated community of concepts which is the contribution of the Aristotelians. The so-called spontaneous groupings of the herbalists are perhaps better understood as attempts to subject the indications afforded by common appellation to the articulation of a larger systematic relationship in which they might be determined unequivocally.

When approached in this way, it is clear that Cæsalpino's contribution to natural history does not consist so much in the originality of his views, as in the distinctness and clarity with

38. Sachs, p. 7.

which he articulates a determinate approach to plant form on the basis of definite principles. It is also clear that this contribution is made in full consciousness of the conceptual background of Aristotelianism then predominant in the universities of northern Italy.[39]

Cæsalpino's complex and conservative version of the Aristotelian conceptual doctrine is found in his *Questionum Peripateticarum*.[40] Cæsalpino defines science as the exposition of being in the function of the universal. Being is exposed by means of its properties, that is, both qualities proper to it, and differences with other being. Such exposition, when considered more closely, falls into three parts: induction, which considers similitude; division, which discovers differences; and definition, which discovers the proper substance of each thing. In other words, science is essentially classification and explanation; being is parsed into its properties; these properties at the same time afford the common marks by which being is classed; in this way classification prepares the way for definition and explanation.[41]

The logical doctrine Cæsalpino presupposes here is well known and does not need detailed presentation. Intellect identifies common marks *(notæ communes)* in comparable objects. By grouping objects on the basis of common marks, and by repeating this grouping at higher systematic levels, a conceptual hierarchy is constituted which reproduces the order of being. Every series of comparable objects has a supreme generic concept which comprehends marks common to all. Beneath the supreme generic concept there are subordinate generic concepts defined by marks common only to some members of the series. The naturalist proceeds from a higher genus to a lower by determination *(determinatio)*, the addition of differentiating marks. He proceeds from a lower genus to a higher

39. On Aristotelian science and method in northern Italy see Ernst Cassirer, "Der Humanismus und der Kampf der Platonischen und Aristotelischen Philosophie," *Das Erkenntnisproblem in der Philosophie und Wissenschaft der neueren Zeit*, I. Band (1911), pp. 73–171; and John Herman Randall, Jr., "The Development of Scientific Method in the School of Padua," *Journal of the History of Ideas* 1 (1940): 177–206, and "The Italian Nature Philosophers," *The Career of Philosophy* (1962), vol. 1, pp. 197–220.
40. Cæsalpino, *Questionum Peripateticorum Libri quinque* (1571). A partial translation with an extensive and useful preface has been made by Maurice Dorolle, *Questions Peripatéticiennes* (1929).
41. Dorolle, transl., pp. 103–106.

by abstraction *(abstractio)*, abandoning limiting marks. The content *(complexus)* and the extent *(ambitus)* of a concept vary inversely; the greater the content, the more marks the concept comprehends, the less its extent; the greater the extent, the more subordinate kinds in which the concept implicates itself, the less its content. The determination of a concept according to the next higher genus and specific differences reproduces the process by which substance unfolds in special forms of being; a complete system of scientific definitions, then, is a complete expression of the substantial forces controlling reality.[42]

It is characteristic both of Cæsalpino's work and of Aristotelian philosophy of the period, however, that while logic is used as the instrument of scientific method, reality is not reduced to logic. The naturalist must always undertake the analysis of material conditions, where only complexes of qualities can define essentially.[43] "But if, " says Dorolle,

42. On Aristotelian conceptual doctrine see Ernst Cassirer, *Substanzbegriff und Funktionsbegriff* (1910), pp. 4–11; Moritz W. Drobisch, *Neue Darstellung der Logik* (1887), §§ 16–26, pp. 17–32; Metzger, pp. 15–34; and Carl Prantl, *Geschichte der Logik im Abendlande*, I. Band (1855), pp. 135, 210 ff.

43. On essential definition see Henri Daudin, *De Linné à Jussieu,* pp. 6–19; O. Hamelin, *Le Système d'Aristote* (1920), pp. 108–152; Jürgen Bona Meyer, *Aristoteles Thierkunde* (1855), pp. 76–102, 330–353, 401–423. Despite the methodological importance of definition, Aristotle's thought on the subject is ambiguous and contradictory, chiefly because it derives from two very different sources: on one hand Aristotle appropriated from Plato's late philosophy a logical instrument of definition ill-suited to the expression of empirical likenesses and differences; on the other hand, Aristotle attributed conceivable being to natural objects and his zoological work implies that the classification of this being would express the relations of the essences. Essential definition in Aristotle's philosophy is not, then, a simple matter. The problems are somewhat clearer when the two sources of his thought on the subject are considered more closely.

Platonic division, Daudin points out, attempts to construct specific concepts by deduction from more general concepts. A thing being proposed, the operation begins with the genus in which that thing is comprehended, and divides the concept as many times as necessary to arrive at a closer determination of the thing's species. At each stage, the procedure opposes antithetical characters without reducing them to negations. The opposed characters divide the whole of the concept and issue in classes equivalent in content and extent. Toward the end of *Timæus* Plato uses habitat as a *fundamentum divisionis* for the animal kingdom, dividing animals in birds, terrestial animals, and aquatic animals (a division which parallels the previous division of elements into earth, air, fire, and water).

Aristotle criticized Platonic division as a logical operation. The procedure, he says, can neither refute a statement, nor draw a conclusion about an accident or property of a thing, nor about its genus (*Analytica Priora*, transl. by A. J. Jenkinson, vol. 1, *The Works of Aristotle* [1928], 1.31.46a;31b.37; *Analytica Posteriora*, transl. by G. R. G. Mure, ibid., 2.5.91b.12–27). Rigorous division, he argues, must distinguish at every step cases in which some character is present and cases in which it is absent, that is, by dividing in accordance with possession and privation (*Categories*, transl. by J. L. Ackrill [1963], chs. 9–10, pp. 31–38. See Hamelin, pp. 137–138, 142–145). In such divisions one class results from the absence of a trait common to the other class, and such a negative determination cannot lead to further divisions, since there can be no specific forms of a negation (*De Partibus Animalium*, transl. by William Ogle, vol. 5, *The Works of Aristotle* [1912], 1.2.643b.21–30; 643a.6–7). The class formed by positive determinations, on the other hand, cannot, as a mere accumulation of determinations, lead to essential knowledge. Man is not essentially defined by the formula "animal, mortal, footed, biped, wingless" (*Anal. Post.* 2.5.92a.1–5; *De Part. Anim.* 1.3.643b.17–23). To attain knowledge of an essence division must proceed by the difference of the difference. With such a procedure the final difference implies all preceding differences, and is at the same time the substance of the thing and its definition (*Metaphysica*, transl. by W. D. Ross, vol. 8, *The Works of Aristotle* [1928], Z.11.1037b.20–24; 12.1038a.9–30). This procedure requires, however, that a single part be decisive, and this is not the case in natural objects. Even if practicable, such division presents a further problem. The genus does not share in specific differences; because the generic concept is independent of its specific differences, it cannot, in any particular case, furnish a "reason" for the existence of one difference rather than another. The irreducibility of the specific to the generic and the generic to the universal, impedes demonstration, in which a conclusion must follow from its premises (*Anal. Post.* 2.5.91b.12–27; *Met.* Z.12.1038a.1–10).

Aristotle's thought on essential definition is not wholly determined by logical considerations. In studying living creatures Aristotle recognized "natural" groups such as birds and fishes whose actual unity had to be respected (*De Part. Anim.* 1.3.643b.9–10; 4.644b.1). If such classes were to be known the naturalist had to account for all the characters which relate or differentiate them (*De Part. Anim.* 1.3.643b.9–10; 643a.24; 4.644a.16; 644b.1; 5.645b.20; *Historia Animalium*, transl. by D'Arcy Wentworth Thompson, vol. 4, *The Works of Aristotle* [1910], 1.6.491a.14; 2.1.497b.9). Here, too, Aristotle distinguished between essential and nonessential definitions (*De Part. Anim.* 1.640b.28; 641a.14; 3.643a.24), and he spoke of the characters on which he based his division of animals as essential (*De Part. Anim.* 4.5.678a.33; 6.682b.27; 13.695b.17).

If we consider only Aristotle's later work, *De Part. Anim.*, the definitive requirements, multiple essential characters, are, with certain qualifications, the data of science are in beings, and in the systems of properties which constitute them, that is, in the singular, we are not far from saying that observation takes precedence over other procedures.[44]

Such an assertion, for an Aristotelian, causes enormous difficulties. If science is predication and the hierarchy of concepts, and if all knowledge is knowledge of universals, what is the status of the concept? Reality is not a concept; reality is being, that which exists in itself, and all being is singular.

---

reconciled in the idea of a functional hierarchy. Every bodily part serves some partial end (*De Part. Anim.* 2.1.646b.12–29), just as the whole body ministers to some sphere of action (*De Part. Anim.* 1.1.642a.11; 1.645b.14–20). Certain actions are inseparable from life, and the parts which serve as instruments of these actions are common to all animals (*DePart.Anim.*1.5.645b.20–646a.2;2.10.655b.29–33;4.5.681b.13–14). Other actions and other parts are proper only to certain genera (*Hist. Anim.* 1.4–5.489a.30–490b.6; 2.1.497b.6–7). The corresponding parts in other genera, however, may have a functional equivalence (*De Part. Anim.* 1.4.644a.12–15; *Hist. Anim.* 1.1.486a.14–487a.10). When we consider the task of the parts rather than the material form, a number of parts which seem at first to exist only in certain animals, exist by analogy in others (*De Part. Anim.* 1.5.645b.8–10; 2.1.647a.19–21; 4.650a.35). At first glance, then, Aristotle seems to establish an equivalence in different functional schemas. His conviction, however, that differences of organization translate functional aptitudes (which form a hierarchy), and that nature creates separate tools for separate tasks, implies a hierarchical arrangement of the animal kingdom which uses multiple, mutually dependent characters in definition (*De Part. Anim.* 2.2.648a.5–9; 4.650b.18–27).

The restriction of definition to bodily parts is, with respect to Aristotle's science, a gross abstraction. Because nature shapes instruments to the task, Aristotle had, in considering function, to consider milieu as well. "Since the body," says Daudin, "exists in view of an action, which is, as final cause, the reason for being of its structure and ordonnance, how could Aristotle, who constantly explains disposition by the function to which it answers, be indifferent to total functioning, necessarily one with the milieu, through which the very actuality of the animal is affirmed?" (*De Linné à Jussieu*, p. 17). In *Hist. Anim..*, Aristotle neither eliminates nor subordinates to anatomical distinctions the additional characters resulting from his various considerations of functional adaptation. The result is not one system, but several, each with a set of "essential" considerations, which, even when taken together, lack logical coherence.

44. Dorolle, transl., p. 11.

> Universals are only in the mind, as signs of reality outside
> it; and outside the mind there is no existence save in singu-
> lars; all the rest is predicated of them.[45]

Cæsalpino solved the problem, at least to his own satisfaction, by identifying thought and reality through the intermediation of imagination. Intellection deals, not with things, but with images. The senses provide images or simulacra of things, which form the matter of any intellectual operation, and comprehension of things is made by the application of the intellect to images. In this way sensation and intellection are related, and there is a unity in the functions of knowledge.

> The human intellect and senses are a unity, as form and
> matter, because they are both participation in the same thing,
> with more or less perfection.[46]

A concept, then, designates the data of the senses and of thought. Concepts are the figures of things as well as of the types by which we class and define them, both εἴδη and εἴδωλα, ideas and emanations of things. Concepts, which are as simulacra in their resemblance to things, are the objects of intellect as well as of sense.[47]

Cæsalpino applied these general principles to the plant kingdom in *De Plantis*. Botany, like all science, is the rapprochement of like, the distinction of unlike, accomplished through distribution in genera and species according to differentiae translating the essences of things.[48]

In working out these essential differences, Cæsalpino began with Aristotle's doctrine of vital unity. Plants are simpler than animals, having a vegetative, but not a sensitive vital principle. There are, however, analogies between plant and animal, since all organic bodies share two functions, nutrition, which tends toward the preservation of the individual, and reproduction, which tends toward the preservation of the kind. All parts of the plant must, in one way or another, be involved in one of these two functions,

45. Ibid., p. 20.
46. Ibid., p. 24.
47. Ibid., p. 25
48. Cæsalpino, *De Plantis Libri XVI* (1583), p. 30.

and all division must rest, therefore, upon the two systems of organs with which these functions are carried out.[49]

Cæsalpino then examines each particular part of the plant, the fundamental organs, root, stem, and leaf, and the temporary organs, flower, fruit, and seed, for their ends or uses in these two vital functions. In his analysis the plant-animal analogy plays an important role, providing a conceptual framework which simultaneously interprets plant morphology part by part, and brings it nearer the common order of experience.[50]

There is, as Sachs says, much that is fantastic and inexact in Cæsalpino's analysis, as well as a great number of sensitive and delicate observations.[51] Perhaps the single most notorious part of Cæsalpino's use of the plant-animal analogy is his treatment of the plant heart *(cor plantarum,* at once *caput radicis* and *germinis principium),*[52] but of course his morphology is not composed entirely of this sort of speculation. He made detailed factual observations of fundamental organs, as well as of accessory organs of special utility; he emphasized development by shoots, which he called *germinatio,* as peculiar to plants; and he acknowledged the distinction of male and female in some species, *Mercurialis, Urtica,* and *Cannabis,* for example. On the other hand, Cæsalpino was unaware of the role of the flower, defining it as a protective device during the formation of fruit, and like Theophrastus, he thought leaves served to shelter the more delicate plant parts from the sun.[53] In arriving at an objective estimate of Cæsalpino's scientific merits, it is important not to overestimate his contributions to morphology. As Agnes Arber points out, the details of *De Plantis* do not advance much beyond Aristotle and Theophrastus.[54] Cæsalpino's organography is important because it established a rationale for deducing the relative importance of plant parts.

49. Ibid., p. 1.

50. Ibid., pp. 3–24.

51. Sachs, p. 51.

52. On *cor plantarum,* see Sachs, pp. 46–47; Agnes Arber, *The Natural Philosophy of Plant Form* (1950), pp. 29–30; and C. E. B. Bremekamp, "A Re-examination of Cæsalpino's Classification," *Acta Botanica Neerlandica* 1 (4); 581–582.

53. See Arber, *Natural Philosophy,* pp. 28–32.

54. Ibid., p. 31.

This notion of importance is, of course, another product of Cæsalpino's Aristotelianism. Division rests upon essential parts, that is, the major functional parts. In plants there are two functions–nutrition and reproduction–and hence two systems of organs–vegetation and fructification. Within each of these systems Cæsalpino calculates the relative importance of each organ by means of an a priori notion of finality. When, for example, we consider the reproductive function, it is clear that what constitutes reproduction is the production of the seed, and accordingly the seed plays an important role in division, while the other reproductive parts, performing subordinate roles, have a subordinate importance in division. The same mode of reasoning holds for the nutritive system. The two chief organs are the root and the stem; of these the root is the superior part because it is prior, answering to the mouth or stomach in animals.[55]

Cæsalpino's classification rests directly upon this deductive procedure. The first function of the vegetative principle is to attract aliment to maintain the life of the individual. In the plant this is a function of the permanent organs, the root and the stem. The first division of plants, then, founded upon but simpler than that of Theophrastus, differentiates woody plants and herbaceous plants. The second function of the vegetative principle is to engender its own kind. Fructification is the most perfect form of reproduction, and Cæsalpino discovers here the richest principle of division.

> There is reason to establish many genera of plants on the production and structure of fruits, since nature employs for the production of no other part of the plant so great a number of different parts.[56]

Cæsalpino then proposes a subdivision of plants using the parts of fructification, describing them in terms of three intrinsic dimensions, number, situation, and figure *(numerous, situs,* and *figura).*[57]

At this point Cæsalpino introduced an equivocation of enormous importance in subsequent classifications. The parts upon

---

55. See A. J. Cain, "Function and Taxonomic Importance," *Systematics Association Publication Number 3* (1959): 5–12.
56. *De Plantis*, p. 27.
57. Ibid., p. 29.

which Cæsalpino's classification rests are functionally important, but the marks or differentiae derived from these parts have little or no importance in the life of plants. C. E. B. Bremekamp, who has dealt at some length with this problem, points out that Aristotle, from whom this classificatory principle derives, confined his interests largely to zoology, and saw no difference between taxonomic and functional importance. Fishes are characterized by their adaptation to life under water, birds by their ability to fly, and so on.

> However, as soon as this principle was applied to plants, it led to difficulties, as indeed it also does, when more rigorously applied to the animal world. This is what Cæsalpino, and afterwards Linné, experienced, and it was in order to save the Aristotelian principle that they made the concession mentioned above: although the characters themselves need not play an important part in the life of the plant, the parts from which they are taken should fulfill this condition. The concession, of course, does not really save the principle, for the functional importance of a part evidently rests on the functional importance of some of its characters, and if the principle was a sound one, those characters that are responsible for the functional importance of the part, should be chosen, not the indifferent ones.[58]

Bremekamp goes on the suggest, and very persuasively, that Cæsalpino's equivocation stems, not from a priori notions, as Sachs believed, but from Cæsalpino's analysis of the material conditions.

In working out his classification practically, Cæsalpino may have begun with either a single "natural" group of plants, or with two or three such groups constituted on general outward appearance. Bremekamp favors the first hypothesis, since it leads to the discovery of a larger number of natural groups, and he has reconstructed such a procedure beginning with the *Liliiflorae*.

Cæsalpino, Bremekamp argues, would early have noted the three-locular fruits, and he would have examined other plants with three-locular fruits. These plants do not form a natural group, but some of them are very similar. These latter possess a single seed in each cell. Cæsalpino would, therefore, have divided these

58. Bremekamp, "A Re-examination," p. 584.

plants in two groups, one with one-seeded fruit cells, and the other with several seeds in each cell. And since the presence of three-locular fruits proved a useful character for diagnosing these groups, Cæsalpino would have turned his attention upon plants resembling one another in the presence of another number of fruit cells. Plants with two-locular fruits, for example, rather naturally divide by the same principles used for three-locular fruits, the presence of one or more than one seed in each fruit cell constituting in this way such well-defined groups as the *Umbelliferæ* and the *Cruciferæ*.[59]

The procedure Bremekamp has outlined, from constitution to theoretical justification, is, as he admits, flawed logically, but not strikingly different from modern practice,

> seeing that the phylogeneticsts of our own time commit the same offense. They too place the theoretical interpretation of their systems, which are arrived at in exactly the same way as those of non-phylogeneticists, in front, and speak of a "phylogenetic method"![60]

Such a procedure, which begins with a small number of natural groups and works out the classification which proved serviceable in those original groups, is too simple always to produce satisfactory results. Also, as Bremekamp notes, the parts from which some marks are taken are not always homologous. For this reason Cæsalpino's system includes many heterogeneous, or "unnatural" groups. This circumstance, in conjunction with the Aristotelian exposition of method, has led to the rather hasty conclusion that abstract speculation cannot elaborate a classification which unites a fundamental principle with groupings justified by natural affinities. The material adduced by Bremekamp tends, at least partially, to refute this old notion. The exposition of classificatory method in *De Plantis* is an attempt to rationalize choices of differentiae after the groups have been constituted on intuitive grounds. The treatise, in other words, is a testimony to the importance which logical justification had for Cæsalpino and his contemporaries, but it can no longer be used as the single most damaging piece of evidence against the artificiality of his system.

59. Ibid., pp. 585–586.
60. Ibid., p. 585.

Whatever the logical lacunae and the unnatural arrangements in Cæsalpino's work, *De Plantis* provided naturalists with an integrated theory which indicated that a rational justification for grouping plant forms was possible. Cæsalpino's speculative physiology, founded upon the Aristotelian conception of vital unity, offered a generally applicable fundamental principle. Using that physiology, Cæsalpino undertook a general analysis of plant forms, subordinating the various parts in relation to functional aims. The general classification of plants worked out on this basis reconciled, although somewhat artificially, observed affinities and speculative principles. In all of these ways Cæsalpino's thought was influential in the development of the systems of nature over the next two centuries.

Cæsalpino's gifts and achievements were closely paralleled in the next generation by those of Joachim Jung, and since Jung studied in Padua in 1618 and 1619, it seems natural to conclude that he was influenced by Cæsalpino's ideas. His main works are the *Logica Hamburgensis* (1635), a representative work in "classical" logic, characterized by radical psychologism;[61] *De Plantis Doxoscopiæ Physicæ Minores* (1662), which treats the principles upon which classification should be founded; and *Isagoge Phytoscopia* (1678), a treatise on plants particularly important for its analysis of plant morphology.

Although Jung's work had no immediate effect upon botany, Jung's morphological ideas, through the medium of John Ray's *Historia Plantarum,* influenced nearly all of the systems of the late seventeenth and eighteenth centuries.[62] Yet it is difficult to estimate

61. An excerpt "On Falsehood and Truth" is printed in Dagobert D. Runes, *The Classics in Logic* (1962), pp. 418–432. Further extracts, analyses, etc. in Hans Kangro, *"Joachim Jungius Experimente und Gedanken fur Begründung d. Chemie als Wissenschaft"* (Wiesbaden: Fr. Steiner, 1968).

62. "Here may be found the principal discoveries made by Cæsalpinus, Columna, Grew, Malpighi, and Jungius in addition to those made by Ray himself; in this way resulted the most complete treatise which had yet appeared on vegetation in general; and it must be remarked that, although this work may not have been very frequently quoted, yet it is through it that the doctrines of these authors were made common and became as it were popular in the science; and on this account we believe that the best monument that could be erected to the memory of Ray would be the republication of this part of his work separately. These writings formed

adequately the nature of Jung's achievement. He is credited with the philosophical rejection of the Theophrastian division of plants into trees and herbs (also occasionally credited to Rivinus), but since this division, although scarcely philosophical, was retained until the time of Linnæus, this does not seem a lasting achievement. In his morphological work, Jung's concise aphoristic method does not, as Agnes Arber points out, lend itself to summary, and the presuppositions behind his statements are not readily adduced.[63] Both Sachs and Nordenskiöld have represented Jung as an anti-Aristotelian,[64] but since Jung's morphological work is largely devoted to the production of a complete list of definitions in the Aristotelian manner, it is difficult to credit this belief.

The difficulty in tracing the precise limits of the influence of Jung's morphology on systematics is itself part of a much larger problem. During the seventeenth century plant study specialized; taxonomy, morphology, physiology, and ecology tended more and more to pursue their special paths, and although all parts of plant science were felt to have numerous and necessary relations, a marked separation begins to be noticeable in the various activities. This is notoriously the case in the separate developments of anatomy and systematics. In plant anatomy a number of men entered the field almost at the same time. Working independently, although aware of one another's contributions, Marcello Malpighi, Robert Hooke, and Nehemiah Grew placed the science of anatomy on a new basis in a very short time. Systematists were aware of these developments, and repeatedly attempted to utilize them in their own work, but since they based their classifications largely upon obvious external features in plants, they found it difficult to utilize the results of delicate morphological investigations. Research into flower structure and plant sexuality, clearly of central concern in any classification based upon plant fructification, were overlooked or neglected, often for years on end.

After the publication of the *Pinax* in 1623, a lethargy settled upon systematics, and only in the second half of the seventeenth

---

an epoch in this history of botany." Cuvier and Thouars, *Biographie Universelle* (Paris, 1843) vol. 35, pp. 252–256.

63. Arber, *Natural Philosophy*, p. 33.

64. Sachs, p. 63; Erik Nordenskiöld, *The History of Biology* (New York: Knopf, 1928), pp. 194–195.

century was there again any progress in taxonomy. Robert Morison's *Præludia Botanica* (1669) opened a new and increasingly polemical discussion of system and method. The important figures in this discussion were Robert Morison, John Ray, Augustus Quirinus Rivinus, and Josef Pitton de Tournefort.[65] All four men, and a great many lesser figures, attempted to coordinate and systematize the principles of Cæsalpino, the legacy of natural groups established by the herbalists, and contemporary work in plant morphology. The result has been best described by Henri Daudin.

> They mark the point of departure of a long struggle in which the attempts at systematic classification, more and more actively renewed because of the importance and the increasing complexity of determinations, hurled themselves one after the other at an invincible mental obstacle, which was nothing but the whole of the images [of plant families]. In this struggle all those systems which wished to draw all their characters only from a single part, all the methods which draw their characters from several parts, but choose them and subordinate them at will, thus remaining more or less artificial, are broken up more or less completely. Since, however, they arise from a need keenly felt, or rather, from a pressing exigency of botanical investigation, and because the abstract combination which rules their march is by its very nature susceptible to many corrections, they never ceased to reform themselves and to derive profit from their checks. For as long as necessary the hierarchy of characters can fortify itself by additions, make itself supple by suppressions, redress itself by new distinctions in such a way as to amend more or less completely this or that arbitrary union or separation which had, quite justly, led to its condemnation.[66]

Viewed with a distant and unsympathetic eye, this protracted struggle appears as one of the comedies of the human intellect. The presuppositions which underlay this struggle tended to reduce the quarrel over system and method to a disagreement about the

---

65. See especially John Ray, *Methodus Plantarum Nova* (1682); *Historia Plantarum Species* (1686); *Synopsis methodica stirpium britannicarum* (1696).

    Of Josef Pitton de Tournefort, see *Elemens de Botanique*, and *Institutiones Rei Herbariæ* (1719).

66. Daudin, *De Linné à Jussieu,,* p. 27.

choice of differential characters. There was no disagreement about the system of nature—its form was known in outline. There was no disagreement about the elements of order—these were visual or tactile qualities, immediately apparent. There was no disagreement about the method used to exhaust that order—it supposed only the variety of plant forms and the ability of the naturalist to select features common to several of them. And yet, despite the persuasive effect of these *idées frustes*, no one quite managed to discover the natural method.

This is a rather superficial view of this continuing struggle, perhaps inevitable as long as one focuses upon methodological directives and systematic results. Admittedly, the great achievement of the period was laborious compilation. This compilation, however, stabilized the tensions set up by theoretical requirements, scientific traditions, technical factors, and professional needs long enough to set the past in order, and to provide a method and a mass of coordinated facts basic to the development of the science. The integrity of the period is best measured, not against its repeated failure to achieve the natural method, but against its discussions of the problems involved in essential definition, category stabilization, and class structure.

As we have seen, naturalists had, by the end of the sixteenth century, appropriated the two chief structural ideas of Aristotelian science, the hierarchy and continuity of natural forms. These two ideas, incompletely worked out and vaguely related to one another, were represented in the single commonplace image, the chain of being. "It is necessary," says Leibniz,

> that all the order of natural beings form but a single chain,
> in which the various classes, like so many rings, are so closely
> linked one to another that it is impossible for the senses
> or the imagination to determine precisely the point at which
> one ends and the next begins.[67]

In terms such as these the figure was universally used in the seventeenth century, and its two points of comparison were well known. If we exclude troublesome speculation about possible worlds and

67. Leibniz, *Hauptschriften zur Grundlegung der Philosophie*, II (1906), p. 558.

man's middling state, naturalists, in applying the figure to nature, meant what contemporary metaphysicians meant. The objects in nature form a hierarchy; there are well-defined qualitative differences which permit the resolution of natural objects in clear-cut classes. At the same time, the objects in nature form a continuum; nature passes from the inanimate to the animate by degrees so fine we discern her transitions with difficulty.

These two seemingly irreconcilable ideas have, as almost every student of Aristotle observes, both theoretical and practical sources. The idea of hierarchy, for example, is a product of Aristotle's doctrine of concepts as well as a close absorption in observed fact. The conceptual doctrine, as Hamelin shows, combines an almost Platonic conception of objects, disengaging the type from its diverse representations, with a procedural method, accomplishing the progressive or regressive passage from the particular to the universal, or from the complex to the simple.[68] Such a doctrine encourages thinking in terms of a hierarchy of clear-cut classes. But as Ross has also shown, natural and geometrical forms offer many examples of classifications in the nature of things, and Aristotle adduces many examples in the *Organon* and in the *Historia Animalium*.[69]

The sources of Aristotle's idea of continuity offer a similar example of miscegenation. In the *Categories* Aristotle says that many quantities, temporal and spatial, are continuous, not discrete.[70] His thought on qualities, as Lovejoy points out, is less clear, but Aristotle observed that any division of objects on a fundamental principle would issue in a linear series of classes offering, not clear-cut distinctions, but shadings and overlappings.[71]

The persuasive effect of these two complex ideas on naturalists from the sixteenth through the eighteenth centuries was such, says Daudin, that they seemed at the time the very formulation of the task of science.[72] Overwhelmed by the sheer variety of natural forms, naturalists adapted the idea of a natural hierarchy to the

68. Hamelin, pp. 76–79.

69. Aristotle, *Selections, ed. W. D. Ross* (1927), pp. ix–x.

70. *Categories*, 4b.20–5a.5.

71. Lovejoy, p. 56.

72. Daudin, *De Linné à Jussieu*, pp. 19–20. "From Aristotelian science there are, then, two ideas, very differently elaborated and, candidly speaking, quite weakly tied to one another, which natural history at the Renaissance received as a heritage. The first is that of a hierarchy of beings: a philo-

systematic inventory of all natural objects. The idea of continuity, on the other hand, tended at first to reduce the idea of system to a practical, but artificial arrangement; later, the idea led to the formation of the natural method. Practically and theoretically these ambiguous and complex ideas played important roles in seventeenth-century natural history, and it is important, therefore, to consider their effects in detail.

The use of the idea of a class hierarchy in sixteenth- and seventeenth-century natural history is best understood in relation to certain limited professional requirements, one of which was the manipulation of conventional signs in order to discover plant names. These names, which often sound to the modern reader as if they possessed some intrinsic value, in reality furnished access to a large body of information about individual plants' organization, history, properties, and uses. Like the virtual knowledge of encyclopedias, this information was accessible only when the plant name was known. For this reason systems are repeatedly described throughout the period as instruments for relating plant specimens to their proper names.[73] A system was an arrangement by which the variety of plant forms, grouped upon some fundamental principle, distributed plant forms in smaller and smaller fractions, and reduced the unmanageable variety of these forms to a body of knowledge in which the old forms and facts were readily accessible, and to which the new might readily be added. "The number and variety of plants," says Ray,

---

sophic dogma which Christian theology, following Neo-Platonism, often took as a theme for a wholly speculative interpretation of the universe, but scarcely suited, in the state of extreme abstraction in which it remained, to determine in a positive fashion a serial classification of what was known through observation of types of animals and plants. The second is that which posits among natural beings insensible and quasi-continuous transitions: this idea, although it may seem to carry less metaphysical weight, has the great advantage of finding in the consideration of sensible objects themselves the appearance of facile verification. Nor does this hinder one, moreover, from deriving from scholastic logic an axiom proper to confer upon it rational necessity: there cannot be in the world such as it is ordered either 'void' or 'dispersion' among 'forms'." Pp. 92–93.

73. Tournefort, for example, equated science with the determination of given plants. "To know plants is precisely to know the names one has given them in relation to the structure of some of their parts." *Elemens*, p. 1.

inevitably produce a sense of confusion in the mind of the student: but nothing is more helpful to clear understanding, prompt recognition and sound memory than a well-ordered arrangement into classes, primary and subordinate.[74]

Some of the period's working assumptions about system and method are revealed by persistent figurative expressions. A system, according to the most commonplace comparison, was a well-ordered army, for if the naturalist did not distribute plants in their divisions, necessarily everything was disordered in confusion and agitation.[75] Another persistent source of parallels was the comparison of method to cryptography. Natural forms were a cryptogram; method was a key to the formative factor in that cryptogram, extracting, isolating, and giving explicit form to something given implicitly in complex relations.[76] The comparison of method to cryptography rested upon the unexpressed belief that a method founded upon the similarities of natural objects isolated and gave expression to the elements of order which controlled reality. The condensation of essentials facilitated the study of plants by exhibiting the elements of order under the most general points of view. The parallel with cryptography suggests, then, the comparison of system to the thread of Ariadne. The mind can comprehend only a few ideas at one time; it is liable to become confused in the labyrinth of nature. To find its way among the complex relations

74. "Præfatio," *Methodus Plantarum Nova*, p. 3.

75. The comparison derives from Aristotle, *Metaphysics* Λ 10.1075a.10: "We must consider also in which of two ways the nature of the universe contains the good and the highest good, whether as something separate and by itself, or as the order of the parts. Probably in both ways, as an army does; for its good is found both in its order and in its leader, and more in the latter; for he does not depend on the order but it depends on him. And all things are ordered together somehow, but not all alike, —both fishes and fowls and plants; and the world is not such that one thing has nothing to do with another, but they are connected." The comparison is used by Cæsalpino, cf. Dorolle, transl., p. 74; Ray, "Præfatio," *Historia Plantarum*, p. 2; and Tournefort, *Elemens de Botanique*, p. 40.

76. The comparison apparently derives from contemporary speculation about the alphabet of human thoughts and the possibility of a universal language or characteristic. See Louis Couturat, *La Logique de Leibniz* (1901), pp. 81–118.

and combinations, thought needs a thread of Ariadne, a palpable sequence of signs to guide and to sustain the mind.[77]

Even in the sixteenth century it was clear that neither practical applications nor factors arising from spatio-temporal situation could furnish a fundamental principle for a generally applicable distribution of plants.[78] By degrees naturalists limited their divisions to characters conceived as intrinsic to plant form, creating classifications based upon various aspects and combinations of roots, stems, leaves, fruits, and flowers. Ready determination required conventional signs discoverable in any plant. No previous knowledge could be supposed. On the other hand, determination had to be founded upon something conceived as inherent in the plant, in the structure, say, easily seen, preferably at one moment, easily discovered in most plants, as constant as possible in a given kind, yet varying from kind to kind, and finally, unequivocal.

Cæsalpino's speculative physiology, based upon the Aristotelian idea of vital unity, seemed to most seventeenth-century systematists to offer both a generally applicable fundamental principle and a viable method of practical characterization.[79] The vital principle of plants involved two functions; these functions, materialized in the vegetative and reproductive system of plants, must operate a division which would readily and infallibly determine plant kinds. Cæsalpino did in fact utilize characters drawn from both the vegetative and reproductive systems of the plant in his system, and he offered both a theoretical and a practical rationale for his practice. Theoretically, he justifies the use of differentiae derived from the

77. Again apparently derivative from Leibniz' *De Arte Combinatoria*. Leibniz also speaks of system as *filum cogitandi* and *filum meditandi*, any procedure which consists in figuring ideas by signs, and their combinations by combinations of signs in such a way that the logical analysis of concepts is replaced by the analysis of characters. See Couturat, pp. 81–118. The comparison was still being used by Goethe in relation to the *Urphänomen*.

78. Ray says there are three standards of classification: first from locality; then from use; then from the likeness of principal parts: root, flower and its cup, seed and its vessel. The first and second are useless; they tear apart what are obviously akin and unite what obviously differ. The third is the best and most congruous with nature. *Methodus Plantarum Nova*, p. 6.

79. "The first so far as I know," says Ray, "to classify plants by the number of seeds and seed-vessels developed from each flower and the position of the *corculum seminale* or point at which germination starts." Ibid., p. 9.

two functional systems because such differentiae express the essence
of the plant;[80] he justifies the practice practically because only
in this way does the naturalist attain sufficient and varied characters
of appreciably equal value suitable to the constitution of plant
groups.[81] In other words, Cæsalpino pretends to determine the
essential properties of a plant, and why these and not other properties are essential; but the kinds of differentiae which he actually
uses in his system form only radical pluralities, not essential nuclei.
Cæsalpino had, as we have seen, hit upon the difference between
taxonomic and functional importance, and in order to save the
principle of essential definition, he was willing to use indifferent
characters rather than characters responsible for the functional importance of the part.

Many instances of this same equivocation can be found in
Cæsalpino's successors. Morison, Ray, Rivinus, and Tournefort re-
fuse to base differentiae on other than structural parts, and all of
them, in one way or another, pretend to penetrate the modifications
and variations of individual plants to discover typical or "essential"
attributes. Ray, for example, repeatedly lists the accidents which
cannot serve in determining true differences in plants; such differences can only derive from the likeness and agreement of the
principal parts, root, flower, cup, seed, and its vessel. "Botanical
descriptions," says Ray,

> often omit or slur over the essential points that decide clas-
> sification, flowers and seeds, calyces and seed-vessels.[82]

80. "We seek out," says Cæsalpino, "similarities and dissimilarities of form, in
which the essence of plants consists, but not of things which are merely
accidents to them." *De Plantis*, p. 27. In 1813 A.-P. de Candolle argued
that a classification based upon either vital function must eventually come
to much the same thing; truly natural classes, established upon one of
the important functions of the plant, are necessarily the same as those
established on the other function. This being so, the naturalist should
choose as the basis for his classification that function with which he
most easily and certainly gained such classes, that is, reproduction. Augustin-Pyrame de Candolle, *Théorié élémentaire de la Botanique* (1844), pp.
66–67.
81. *De Plantis,* p. 27: "We are right to establish many genera on the production
and structure of the fruits, since nature employs in the production of
no other part so great a number of different pieces."
82. *Methodus Plantarum Nova*, p. 5.

Yet in defending himself from the criticism of Tournefort, Ray admits that when one peculiar characteristic cannot be found common to a group, the naturalist must admit as many attributes as possible common to the whole group.[83] Tournefort, too, who proposed to define genera by essential marks drawn from fruit and flower, eventually admitted that,

> it is a question of finding expedients in order to distinguish the genera of plants with all possible distinctness, and if the lesser of their parts are more suitable for this than those which we call the most noble, we must prefer them without difficulty.[84]

Taken at face value these remarks can be read as attempts to stabilize the generic and specific concepts.[85] The expedients of which Tournefort speaks are neither opportune formulae nor indications of the Creator's intention; they are observable, objective characters inherent in the plant's structure. The genera, he argues in *Elemens de Botanique,* are imprinted with "a character common

83. Charles E. Raven, *John Ray Naturalist, His Life and Works* (1942), pp. 290–291.

84. *Elemens*, p. 26.

85. Generic and Specific taxa in the systems of the sixteenth century were not unequivocally related to determinate and constant empirical criteria. In Aristotle, the two group designations are γένος and εἶδος. γένος is used for the nine major classes in Aristotle's treatment of animals; εἶδος is not (J. B. Meyer, *Aristoteles Thierkunde* (1855), p. 345 f.). In subordinate groups γένος and εἶδος are used almost interchangeably (*Hist. Anim.* 1.6.490b.17; 4.7.532b.14; 5.30.556a.14; 9.19.617a.11–617b.16). γένος is the more general and numerous term, the usual designation of a main group in relation to a subordinate group (*Hist. Anim.* 1.1.486a.23; 1.6.490b.31; 4.7.531b.21; *De Part. Anim.* 1.4.644a.31; 4.5.679a.15). The terms cannot, however, be precisely understood as genus and species (see D. M. Balme, *Classical Quarterly* 12 (1): 81–98). Aristotle had no set criteria, either for γένη or εἴδη; in general the larger groups he distinguished on the basis of analogy, the smaller groups on the basis of likeness or difference of form (J. B. Meyer, p. 345 f.). He did assert that through division of γένη we arrive finally at specific indivisibles, the basic units of science (*De Part. Anim.* 1.4.644a.29–33). He did not, however, draw up a list of such units for any one genus, and he did not always carefully distinguish congeners (Daudin, *De Linné à Jussieu*, p. 18). In short, Aristotle seems to have made no attempt to relate genus and species regularly, either to one another, or to any general defining criteria.

to each of their species which should serve us as a guide in ranging them in their natural place"; the naturalist could not disregard these marks of distinction "without departing very visibly from the truth."[86] And once the genera were established and their common features noted genus by genus, they might in turn be collected in larger groups, which also actually existed, and could be defined by means of common marks in either flower or fruit which united several genera. Similarly, Ray, for all his equivocations, bases the arrangement of his "genera" (that is, the large groups or orders), *species subalternæ* (or genera) and *species infimæ* (or species) upon a selection of objective characters which did least violence to recognized affinities in plant forms.

If we take these various choices of classifying criteria as attempts at essential definitions, we shall only be convinced, as Ernst Mayr says, how arbitrary are the methods of determining the essential natures of organisms.[87] In the systems of the seventeenth century, however, the practical and the theoretical, as well as observation and speculation are strangely integrated. A fundamental faith in the objective existence of a natural hierarchy leads directly to the identification of natural history with inventory. The inventories are organized very differently, however, and we shall not understand their principles if we lay univocal stress on methodological justifications. The practical need for easy identification, especially at the higher systematic levels, led to a stress on parts which offered a fundamental principle in some complex structure of fairly constant characters. Often coupled with speculation about "essential" or "perfect" parts, this practical necessity led directly to characterization by means of single parts, which in turn led to groups unjustified and unjustifiable by observation of natural affinities. This unstable amalgam of opposing tendencies, of observation and practical determination, lay at the root of systematic instability, and the inability of naturalists of this period to set forth a generally acceptable or applicable system.

The acknowledged faults of these systems—the arbitrary, rigid divisions, the artificial groupings—considered together with the virtues of classification—the abridgement of thought and mnemonic

86. Tournefort, *Elemens*, p. 20.
87. Ernst Mayr, "Theory of Biological Classification," *Nature* 220 (5167): 545–548.

ease, the clarity and order with which relations were presented free of troublesome detail, the point and precision given observation and description—led directly to the conception of a method which would make known the actual relations, organization, and nature of plants, "a method," says Ray, "as perfect as nature permits."[88]

In this conception the Aristotelian idea of continuity, συνέχεια, a series linking natural forms by multiple affinities in a continuous sequence, played a critical role.

As we have seen, the herbalists recognized and established many natural plant groups on the basis of general outward appearance. In such groups a certain structure or general resemblance was so striking, rapprochement was made before the relation could be analyzed. Many plant families—*Coniferæ, Cruciferæ, Graminaceæ,* and *Umbelliferæ,* for example—were established in the sixteenth century, and remained intact throughout the vicissitudes of the struggle over systems. As the study of plants grew more extensive it was recognized that most European plants, which seemed structurally isolated, were members of plant families of which the greater part of the members were exotic. It seemed possible to extend the spontaneous groupings to cover these relations simply on the basis of general appearance. "It was then conceived," says de Candolle,

> that it would be possible to range all well-known plants in natural groups, that is to say, determined by the whole of their organic resemblances, and that such an order would give to him who knew it the most faithful image of all that we know about the structure, and consequently about the history of plants.[89]

Long before this natural method was perfected, its form and function were well known. The *locus classicus* for a statement of its form was Aristotle's *Historia Animalium.*

> Nature proceeds little by little from things lifeless to animal life in such a way that it is impossible to determine the exact line of demarcation, nor on which side thereof an intermediate form should lie.[90]

88. *Methodus Plantarum Nova,* p. 5.
89. A.-P. de Candolle, *Théorie élementaire,* p. 45.
90. *Historia Animalium* 8.1.588b.4–7.

The final end of natural history was to represent this system in each of the three kingdoms of nature, to study the compositions, structures, and relations of natural objects, and to classify them in such a way that the order of nature would be condensed and reproduced in the method. In relation to plant form, the natural method, when perfected, would admit no exceptions, and would be independent of practical interest or value imputed by human will. Comprehending all plant parts, properties, faculties, and qualities, such a method would consider roots, stems, and leaves, as well as flowers and fruits, and draw from the comparison of their resemblances and differences the affinities which resolved them in groups.

Such a natural method is not, as John Ray says, the task of one man or one age.[91] The idea of continuity, however, did have one immediate effect upon classification; it tended to make the whole notion of a hierarchical system appear a convenient but artificial division of natural forms with no counterpart in nature. It is not possible, says Ray, to divide all plants so exactly as to include every species without leaving any in positions anomalous or peculiar; something which would so define each genus by its own characteristics that no species would be left homeless or be found common to many genera.

> Nature does not permit anything of the sort. Nature, as the saying goes, makes no jumps, and passes from extreme to extreme only through a mean. She always produces species intermediate between higher and lower types, species of doubtful classification linking one type with another and having something in common with both—as for example the so-called zoophytes between plants and animals.[92]

Ray does not challenge the notion of fixed natural kinds established by the Author of Nature, but his use of the principle of continuity makes clear the artificiality of the project of distributing plant forms in a hierarchy of mutually exclusive units. If there are no cleavages in nature, our classifications are not hers. Those which we create are relative to our needs and our knowledge. An arrangement into classes, although indispensable to memory, and the surest

91. *Methodus Plantarum Nova*, p. 5.
92. Ibid., pp. 4–5.

means to the determination of plant specimens, has little or nothing to do with those combinations, nuances, and relations which alone establish the natural method. Until the perfection of this method, all systems are necessarily interim arrangements, justified only when congruous with nature, uniting forms obviously akin and dividing forms obviously differing.

Precisely how the seventeenth-century systematists reconciled practical requirements and natural affinities is clear when we examine the systems of Ray and Tournefort.

Ray conceived the *Historia Plantarum* to facilitate learning about plants,

> by so methodising them and giving such certain and obvious characteristic notes of the genera that it shall not be difficult for any man to find out infallibly any plant especially being assisted by the figure of it.[93]

He rejected methods based upon locality and usage, preferring one taken from the likeness and agreement of principal plant parts. Using the Theophrastean division of *arbores, frutices, suffrutices,* and *herbæ* to establish a broad general division of plant forms, Ray ranged within these primary sections his *genera, species subalternæ,* and *species infimæ.* Such a method, he admitted, could not be perfect or complete; there are always ambiguous or anomalous forms.[94]

In using the Theophrastean division Ray discovered his greatest difficulty in distributing the numerous herbs. He first subtracted imperfect plants and plants with a very small seed from their number.[95] The remainder of the herbs he divided into two groups, herbs whose seed-plant is two-lobed, and herbs whose seed-plant is not two-lobed, or rather not possessed of two cotyledons.[96] Within this first subdivision Ray grouped plant families on the basis of their most remarkable traits. In distributing the subordinate genera, Ray held partially with Cæsalpino, drawing differentiae

---

93. *The Correspondence of John Ray,* ed. Edwin Lankester (1848), pp. 160–161.
94. *Historia Plantarum* I, pp. 50–51.
95. Ibid., pp. 51–53.
96. For Ray's early observations on seed leaves, published a year before Malpighi's *Anatome Plantarum* see "Discourse on the Seeds of Plants," *Further Correspondence of John Ray,* ed. W. T. Gunther (1928), pp. 70–77.

from fruit and seed, but using, as the need arose, marks drawn from the flower and its cup, root, and leaves.

Despite its complexity, Ray's division only continued a procedure well-established in the sixteenth century. The most general divisions in his system impose an abstract framework and divide the plants into readily managed sections.[97] Smaller groups or families are worked out within this framework on the basis of the most striking group features. The subordinate genera consist of a few characteristic notes, which are neither diagnoses nor descriptions. Finally, the grouping of species within the genera, and the descriptions of the individual species are carefully done, and the species form the actual basis of Ray's work.[98]

The oppositions by means of which Ray attained his natural groups at various levels, are, despite their appearance, scarcely of logical rigor. They often consist, as Daudin points out, of the presence or absence of an organic detail, of a larger or smaller size with respect to a norm, or of two or more different dispositions of an organ or organs. Ray's synoptic tables differ profoundly in composition from "division" as conceived by Aristotle.

> The care to represent exactly and clearly a certain datum has here already become the ambition to exhaust all the possible combinations among abstract characters: the "method" of the naturalist, oriented by observation, utilizes according to the needs of his project and without too much care for universal rules, the formal instrument which logical culture has prepared for him.[99]

The compromise is, of course, related to Cæsalpino's earlier equivocation upon characters of taxonomic and functional importance. Like Cæsalpino's rather artificial justifications of plant groups, Ray's synoptic tables testify to a desire for and the factual impossibility of a logical rationale in dividing plant forms. Ray was aware that the characters on which he based his division were of little importance in the life of the plant, and his general statements claim only that the groups are based upon the principal parts of the plant.

97. "Herbarum Tabula Generalis," *Historia Plantarum*, pp. 59–60.
98. See Ernst Mayr, "Illiger and the Biological Species Concept," *Journal of the History of Biology* 1 (2): 165–166.
99. Daudin, *De Linné à Jussieu*, pp. 31–32.

Josef Pitton de Tournefort also equated the genuine foundations of botany with the determination of given plants.

> To know plants is precisely to know the names one has
> given them in relation to the structure of some of their
> parts. This structure makes the character which essentially
> distinguishes plants from one another.[100]

The problem of determination, he argued, was best approached
through the genera, which included the common perceptible traits
of the subordinate species. The naturalist's task was to describe
and to name genera on the basis of these common characters.
Considering in detail the five principal parts of the plant, Tournefort proposed a primary division of genera upon the form of
fruit and flower, and a secondary division, for surer distinction,
on other, vegetative differences, reasoning that,

> the flower and the fruit are parts absolutely necessary to
> establish all the genera whose species bear flowers and fruits;
> but that these parts are not sufficient to distinguish those
> genera from one another.[101]

Once the genera were established and their common features noted
genus by genus, they were in turn collected in larger groups in
such a way that the whole of the science might be taken in at
a glance. The principles used to establish the genera served equally
for the higher groups. These groups existed, according to Tournefort, and the task of the naturalist was the discovery of common
marks in either flower or fruit which united several genera.

> All the investigations which I have made in examining the
> different manners in which one might compose those classes
> have convinced me that their composition is not arbitrary,
> but is a consequence of the previous resolution in regard
> to genera, and that one must respect the real relations which
> are found amongst them; that is to say, the relations drawn
> from the structure of their essential parts, which are the
> flower and the fruit.[102]

100. *Elemens*, p. 1.
101. *Elemens*, p. 30.
102. *Elemens*, p. 40.

In grouping genera, Tournefort specified that recorded genera were not to be dismembered nor common marks emphasized which brought together very disparate genera. Having made these two concessions to order justified by natural affinities, Tournefort established the higher taxa of his system upon plant parts in which he found a complex structure of constant characters. He based his classes on floral characters, on the presence or absence of flowers, on petaled or apetalous flowers, on simple and composite flowers, on simple mono- and polypetalous flowers, on regular and irregular flowers, on the form of the corolla, and on the constitution of composite flowers. Tournefort formed his sections on the relative situation of fruit and flower, on the number of cells in fruits, on the constancy of fruits, upon particularities of corolla and seeds, and upon the presence or absence of the calyx. This almost exclusive focus upon the flower in classification brought together genera of very different character. In other words, the practical determination of plant genera prevailed over the presentation of natural affinities in the higher categories of Tournefort's system. Tournefort could only justify the classes of his system on the grounds of commodity:

> it is necessary to remark that whatever method one uses, and however exact it may be, one will always believe it defective if one wishes to call faults certain combinations which at first appear insupportable.[103]

It is by means of such compromises that Tournefort and his contemporaries were able to reconcile practical requirements and natural affinities. Their systems were quite frankly practically necessary interim arrangements.

Important as the distinction between an artificial system and the natural method may have seemed to these naturalists, neither system nor method would have been possible without the common, unstated belief in the objective reality of a hierarchy of natural forms. This belief, and the qualitative, finalist method to which it gives rise, have often been interpreted as anachronistic survivals of Aristotelian science. In broad outline this position is unassailable: as we have seen, few of the conceptual elements in natural history

103. *Elemens*, p. 42.

from the sixteenth through the eighteenth century are original, and many of them derive from Aristotle. But this is an Aristotelianism singularly inclined toward the modern spirit, stressing the claims of experience and material conditions against those of tradition and authority. And although logical organization gives the external form to rational explanation, reality is by no means reduced to logic. The problems posed are no longer, except in form, pure problems of essence; the naturalist seeks out the structure of fact, and description has an increasingly important role in his discussions.

This brief anatomy of the problem of order as it was received and understood by the systematists of the late seventeenth century reveals two main tendencies. The problem of order originated in limited professional requirements, the most important of which was the choice and manipulation of conventional signs proper to discover plant names. This practice allowed the naturalist to establish relations between plant specimens and assembled information about properties and uses of a particular plant and about other plants of the same genus. The need for easy identification of plant specimens, however, led naturalists to emphasize visible parts which offered a complex structure of constant characters, and to use the larger systematic classes as means of access to the solidly established genera and species. Through a kind of logic inherent in the systems with which the practical requirement was carried out, however, naturalists were led toward the conception of a method which would do justice to the affinities actually observed in plants, not only at the level of genera and species, but at the higher echelons, at the levels of classes and orders as well.

Linnæan thought was imbued with these inherited professional contradictions. On one hand Linné defined a "true" botanist as one who had a notion of botany which proceeded from the "genuine" foundations and knew how to name all plants with an intelligible name.[104] He equated the genuine foundation of botany with the determination of given plants, and regarded it as a certain truth, that all solid erudition and true natural knowl-

104. *Philosophia botanica* (1751), § 7, p. 4.

edge depended upon knowing the species.[105] A system, in Linné's opinion, was founded in the need for practical determination. By using a formal hierarchy the naturalist could attain or insert particular plants in the system of nature. Let, says Linné, any unknown Indian plant be presented to a botanophile who understands no system:

> the botanophile will turn over all descriptions, figures, and indexes in vain, nor shall he at last find out the plant unless it be by mere chance.[106]

The mind, grasping but a small number of ideas, wants a support, a certain method of conduct, which allows thought to pursue a palpable progress. Given such a method, says Linné,

> The systematist can soon determine whether it be a genus which is already known, or whether it be a new genus.[107]

In the *Critica botanica* Linné speaks of descending the key of the system from higher groups to a particular genus, and of system and method as giving the genera and species ranged under them. System, says Linné, referring to this regular and infallible resolution, is the thread of Ariadne without which the science of botany remains a chaos.[108] These limited, professional considerations explain as well the contrast of the philosophic titles of *Fundamenta Botanica, Critica botanica,* and *Philosophia botanica* with their prescriptive, pedantic, even oracular content: in these works Linné sets forth a body of procedures which will allow naturalists to establish in a controlled and practical way likenesses and differences in plant specimens.

105. Ibid., § 256, p. 202: "A young botanist should know all the classes: a candidate should be acquainted with all the genera; and a master of the science should know the greatest part of the species. The greater number of species he knows, so much the better botanist he is. And it is a certain truth, that all solid erudition and true natural knowledge depends upon knowing the species."
106. Ibid., § 156, p. 98.
107. Ibid., § 156, p. 98.
108. *The Critica Botanica of Linnæus,* transl. Sir Arthur Hort (1938), § 284, pp. 163–164.

But Linné also recognized very early in his career that a system founded upon conventional marks could not do justice to observable affinities. The aim of the Linnæan system of classification according to stamens and pistils, access to plant names through inspection of the plant itself, was admittedly artificial. But Linné produced as well the fragments of a "natural" method, and he declared repeatedly that the final end of botany was to complete this method, to study the compositions, structures, and relations of plants, and to classify them in such a way that the order of nature was condensed and reproduced in the method.[109]

Perhaps the most important single question to be asked in relation to the work of Linnæus, or any other eighteenth-century naturalist, is, how have practical disposition and natural affinities been reconciled in theory and in practice, for the question involves eventually nearly every assumption underlying eighteenth-century natural history, the system of nature, the elements of order, and the representation of that order. What follows is an analysis of the conflict between these two tendencies in the work of Carl von Linné, an attempt to show how these tendencies complemented, contrasted, and combined with one another at every level of the Linnæan system.

109. See "Præfatio," *Genera plantarum* (1737), unpaginated; *Classes plantarum opus denuo editum, Skrifter af Carl von Linné* (1907), pp. 484, 487; *Philosophia botanica,* § 77, p. 27; *Cui bono?, A.A.,* vol. 3, §§ 12, 14, pp. 249, 254.

Chapter II

CLASSES AND ORDERS

On the twenty-third of December, 1729, a dissertation entitled "Deo Duce! ΓΑΜΟΣ ΦΥΤΟΝ sive NUPTIAE ARBORUM" was defended at Uppsala. The author and præses was the university librarian, Georg Wallin. The dissertation was an unoriginal *akademisk snilleprof,* a compilation of citations from ancients and moderns who had treated aspects of the traditional analogy between plants and animals.[1] Linné, then a student at Uppsala, had long considered a system of classification based upon the sexual parts of plants.[2] Linné was not given an opportunity to act as opponent to the Wallin dissertation. He wrote instead the *Præludia sponsaliorum plantarum,* in which he set forth a botanical version of the sexes of plants.[3] This paper, written at the age of twenty-two, is a curious example of Linnæan thought and repays close study.

The *Præludia* began by recalling ways in which the analogy between plants and animals had been approached. Linné then drew attention to the reproduction of plants by means of their own fruit. Using the plant-animal analogy to analyze the problem of plant reproduction into accepted truths, Linné deduced from principles attained in this way the consequence he had already foreseen: the generative organs constitute the "most essential" parts of the

1. See the note by Th. M. Fries in *Valda smärre skrifter af botaniskt innehåll, Skrifter af Carl von Linné* 4 (1908), pp. 23–24.
2. For the traditional view see *Vita Caroli Linnæi, Carl von Linnés självbiografier,* ed. Elis Malmeström and Arvid Hj. Uggla (1957), p. 98. For a corrected version see Uggla, "Linné och Linnéanerne," *Ny illustrerad svensk litteraturhistoria,* 2. delen (1956), pp. 202–205.
3. Reprinted in *Skrifter af Carl von Linné,* 4, pp. 1–26.

flower. In plants all reproduction takes place by way of fruit. There must, therefore, be generative organs, for from the animal kingdom it is known that all issue requires male genitalia to impregnate the egg, and nature, Linné added, is very simple and nearly always constant.[4] In the plant kingdom there is no fruit without flower, just as there is no issue in the animal kingdom without previous congress. Since the flower is as much a necessary antecedent to fruit as genital organs to issue, it follows necessarily that within the flower the organs of generation must be found, and that those parts with the rudiments of fruit, on the analogy with the animal kingdom, must be female, those with apices male.[5]

Linné analyzed the six parts of the flower—calyx, petal, stamen, apex, pistil, and fruit—with respect to constancy, rejecting the floral envelopes because they are not inseparable from fructification.[6] Stamen, pistil, and fruit, however, are always present, albeit in three ways. Most plants contain in one flower both stamens and pistils. Some plants, however, have two distinct kinds of flower on one stalk, some of which have stamens and apices without pistils, some with pistils alone; the former are sterile, the latter fertile. Finally, there are other plants upon some of which are found flowers with apices but not pistils, while upon others there are pistils without apices, the former sterile, the latter fertile; yet both grow from one kind of seed, which is to say, they are not separate species.

Linné used these three combinations to establish a tripartite division of plants which he justified with numerous examples and the authority of Tournefort.[7] By means of this correlation of speculation and experience Linné reached the "most essential" parts of the flower; he showed the organs of generation to be inherent in the structure of plants; and he satisfied himself that these parts are universal. He went on to compare the organs of plant reproduction with the terminology of animal sexuality adopted by Vaillant. Directly following this equation Linné rose for a moment above the rather dry and scholastic conduct of his argument into the poetry inherent in his comparison.

---

4. *Præludia sponsaliorum plantarum*, §§ I–VII, pp. 8–10.
5. Ibid., §§ VI–VII, p. 10.
6. Ibid., §§ VIII–X, pp. 10–11.
7. Ibid., §§ XI–XIV, pp. 11–13.

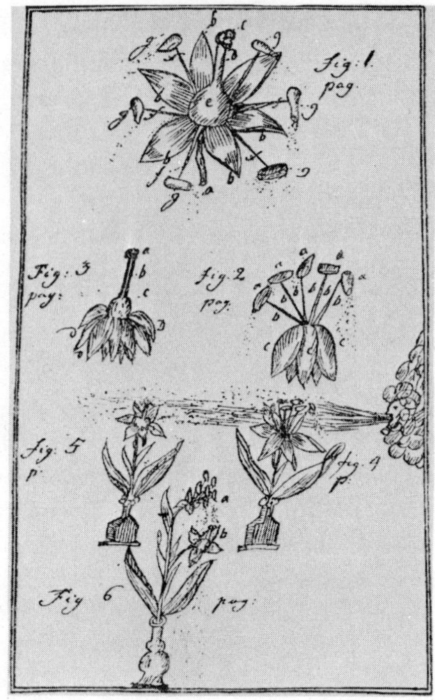

Linné's illustration for *Præludia Sponsaliorum Plantarum*.

Explicatio figurarum.

Fig. 1. Flos *Androgynus* s. Hermaphroditus.

    a. petiolus.

    b. petala s. *Thalamus.*

    c. corolla pistilli s. *Vulva*, infundibulum.

    d. Pistillum, stilus s. *Vagina*, Tuba.

    e. fructus, capsula s. *Ovarium.*

    f. stamina s. *vasa spermatica.*

    g. apices s. *Testiculi.*

Fig. 2. *Flos masculinus.*

    a. apices, *Testiculi.*

    b. stamina, *Vasa spermatica.*

    c. petala et. calyx; *Thalamus.*

Fig. 3. *Flos foemininus.*

    a. *vulva*, corona styli.

    b. *vagina, Tuba;* pistillum.

    c. ovarium, fructus rudimentum.

Fig. 4. *Planta mas*, florem in diversa planta a fructu præbens.

Fig. 5. *Planta foemina*, tota planta a masculina distincta.

Fig. 6. Planta flore (a) a fructu (b) separato in eadem planta.

> The flowers' leaves themselves (:petala:) contribute nothing
> to generation, but only do service as bridal beds which the
> great Creator has so gloriously arranged, adorned with such
> noble bed curtains, and perfumed with so many soft scents
> that the bridegroom with his bride might there celebrate
> their nuptials with so much the greater solemnity. When
> now the bed is so prepared, it is time for the bridegroom
> to embrace his beloved bride and offer her his gifts; I mean,
> then one sees how the testicula open and powder the pul-
> verem genitalem, which falls upon the tubam, and fertilizes
> the ovarium.[8]

Linné then resumed his argument and considered the process of
fertilization, examining two theories, that of Samuel Morland and
that of Leeuwenhoek. Showing that neither theory can be correct,
Linné demonstrated with seven practical experiments that fertilization occurs, though how it occurs was impossible to reconstruct.[9]
After demonstrating likenesses between plant and animal egg, Linné
concluded his essay with observations on the cotyledons, or *hjärt-
blad*, so-called on their analogy with the animal placenta.[10]

Despite the hesitancies and lacunæ one can scarcely exagger-
ate the importance of the *Præludia* in Linné's systematic work.
It is essential, therefore, to keep in mind the chief ideas which
served as starting points for his subsequent research. Linné accepted
without question the scientific tradition stemming from Cæsalpino,
which sought the basis of classification in the reproductive function
of plants, ascribing the essence of the plant to the parts of fructification. Within the reproductive system, Linné traced the most essential parts of the flower to the stamens and pistils by means of
a priori reasoning: since the function of reproduction is essentially
one of fertilization, the organs of fertilization are clearly more
important than the floral envelopes which enclose them. Linné
found parts which fulfill the requirements of systematic classification: the sexual organs are inherent in plant structure; they are
always present; and their use requires no comparative knowledge.
Finally, by surveying the entire reproductive process, Linné laid
down the lines for his later work on the natural method.

8. Ibid., § XVI, p. 14.
9. Ibid., § XVIII, p. 15.
10. Ibid., §§ XIX–XXIX, pp. 15–19.

Linné's next problem was a closer analysis of parts involved in plant reproduction. The plant-animal analogy threw light upon the general features of the process of generation. Linné needed now to discover under what aspects the most essential parts of the flower, the stamens and pistils, were as constant as possible in a given plant, yet varied sufficiently from plant to plant to operate a general division of the kingdom. Linné's reflections on classification during 1730 and 1731 are found in the five successive modifications of the *Hortus Uplandicus* and the *Adonis Uplandicus*.[11] These *örteböcker,* or descriptive plant lists, resulted from Linné's attempts to acquaint himself with plants encountered in botanical literature and from his demonstrations at the University gardens. In *Hortus Uplandicus 1* Linné distributed 454 plants according to Tournefort's system, appending synonyms, short observations, and remarks on leaf and floral form. C. A. M. Lindman, in his patient study of these papers, noted that Linné occasionally hit upon more pregnant or essential specific differences than those cited from botanical literature, and that among these some offer clues to Linné's scientific preoccupations.[12] In *Hortus Uplandicus 2* Linné distributed 417 plants using Tournefort's system. Linné, however, made some changes. The class *Arbore Apetali* was dropped, and the member plants were relegated to the *Amentacei.*[13] Class members were shifted about the better to reveal their "natural" relations. Of the *Cerinthe*, for example, which he placed among the *Infundibuliformes*, Linné remarked,

> This without any reason Tournefort has placed among the
> bell-shaped, although nature has so carefully fastened it to-
> gether with the rough-leaved (among the tunnel-shaped).[14]

The notations of stamen number found in *Hortus Uplandicus 1* were continued.[15] And finally, Linné undertook a new division of the *Umbellatæ*. His descriptive remarks again reveal his classifica-

11. Four of these are printed in *Carl von Linnés ungdomsskrifter*, saml. Ewald Åhrling (1888), pp. 109–360.
12. C. A. M. Lindman, "Carl von Linné såsom botanist," *Carl von Linnés betydelse såsom naturforskare och läkare* (1907), pp. 10–11.
13. *Ungdomsskrifter*, 1. ser., pp. 198–199.
14. Ibid., p. 164. Other arrangements are listed in Lindman, pp. 11–12.
15. Ibid., pp. 165–166.

Plates

HORTUS
CLIFFORTIANUS

Carl von Linné.

The title page from *Hortus Cliffortianus*. The symbolism has been interpreted by W. T. Stearn: "A crowned goddess, Mother Earth or Cybele, sits upon a lion and lioness symbolic of her power; in one hand she holds a pair of keys indicating her right to the garden at any time; at her feet are a pot of *Cliffortia*, a plan of the Hartekamp garden and two cherubs, one explaining Linnæus's centigrade thermometer. A negress brings her an *Aloe* from Africa, an Arabian woman a plant of *Coffea arabica* from Asia, a befeathered American Indian a plant of *Hernandia* from America. On the pedestal behind her stands a Janus-like bust wreathed with *Kæmpferia*, etc., the bearded head possibly portraying Clifford, against a background of topiary work. On the right overtopping all else is a banana in flower and fruit to indicate Linnæus's success in its cultivation at Hartekamp. A handsome young god, Apollo, steps forward below it, bringing light in his right hand and with his left hand casting aside the shroud of darkness around the goddess; he wears a wreath of laurel, and his face is the face of young Linnæus; underfoot he tramples the dragon of falsehood, slain with one of his arrows, an obvious reference to the counterfeit hydra at Hamburg exposed as a fraud by Linnæus while on his way to Holland. [The illustration] thus graphically expresses Linnæus's own opinion of his place in botany."

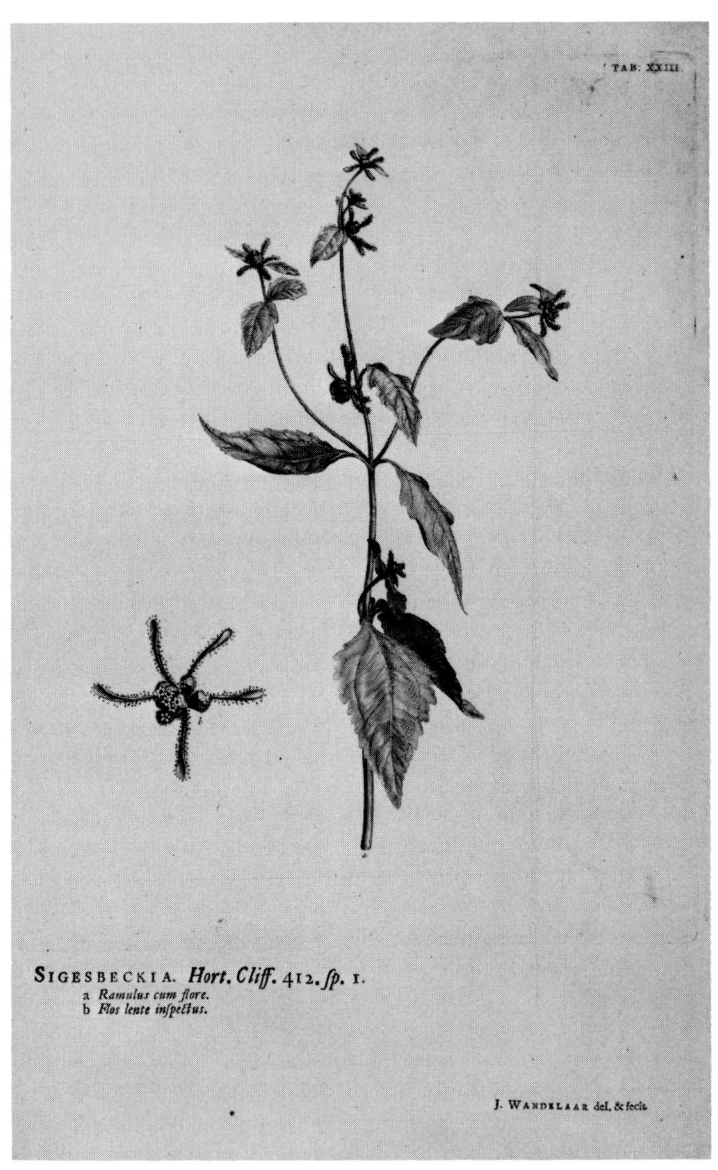

Sigesbeckia from the *Hortus Cliffortianus*. "Johann G. Siegesbeck is remembered today only through the unpleasant small-flowered weed which Linnæus named *Sigesbeckia*."

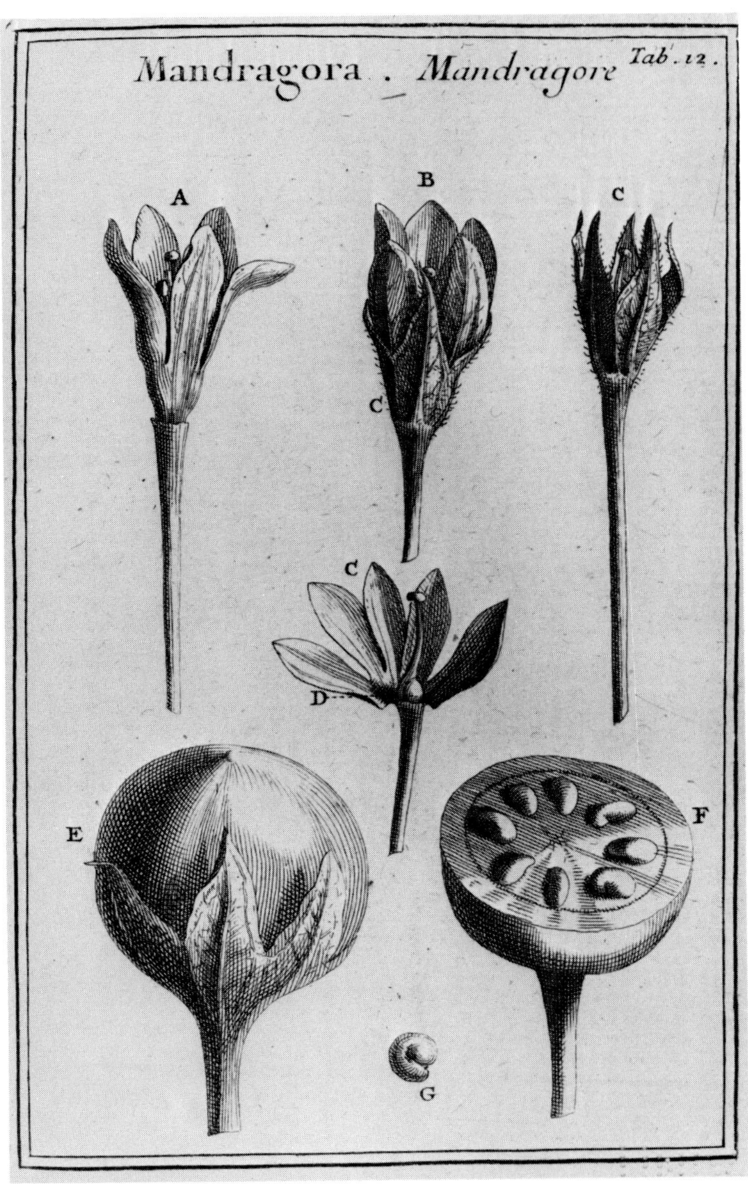

Mandragora from Tournefort's *Institutiones*.

Belladona.

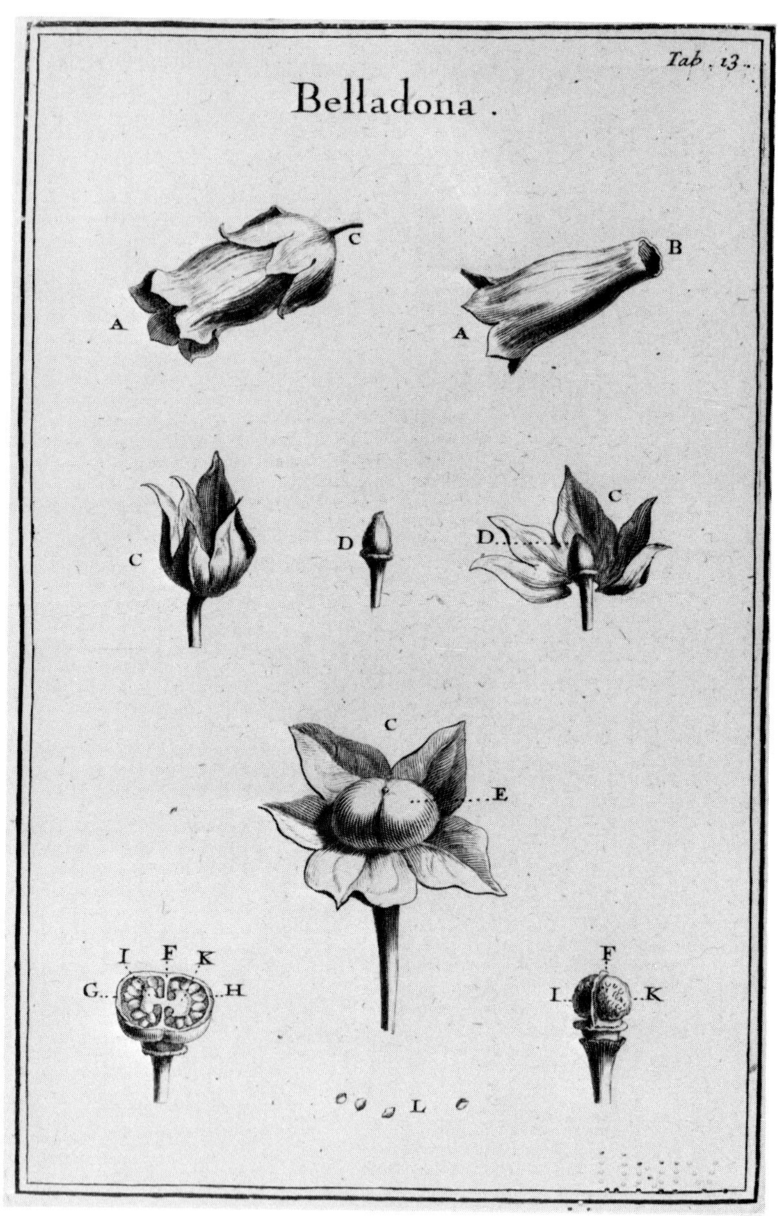

Belladona from Tournefort's *Institutiones*.

Heliocarpus from *Hortus Cliffortianus*. "Who could ever behold an almost round fruit; bordered with a halo of rays, without thinking of the Sun, as conceived by the painters?"

Hernandia from *Hortus Cliffortianus.* "*Hernandia* is an American tree, with the handsomest leaves of any, and less conspicuous flowers—from a botanist who had supreme good fortune, and who was highly paid to investigate the natural history of America: would that the fruits of his labours had corresponded to the expenditure."

tory interests. He listed, for example, the following characteristic notes for this group:

> 1. *Flower,* 5 unequal, nude petals, 2. *Stamens* 5, 3. *Pistil* duplex, bent en dehors, 4. *Fruit* with two naked seeds underneath the flower.[16]

The changes in terminology and description are greatest, however, in the last three revisions of the *Hortus Uplandicus.* Here Linné attempted for the first time to stabilize the species concept and to rationalize botanical nomenclature. Even more important, however, Linné undertook a general classification based upon the method "which is shown in my Nuptiis plantarum."[17] In *Hortus Uplandicus* 4 and *Adonis Uplandicus,* both dating from 1731, the system was broadened to include twenty-four classes.[18]

During the years immediately following, Linné made his journey to Lapland where he discovered "diverse plants, which no botanist had seen previously,"[19] and to Holland where he made the acquaintance of "an infinite quantity of African and Indian plants."[20] Any defects in the classificatory system which resulted from narrow acquaintance with north European plants were modified through this experience of tropical and arctic flora. This prolonged adjustment of speculative principles and wide-ranging experience issued in a flexible, ingenious, and precise instrument of classification, the *Clavis Systematis Sexualis,* which Linné published in 1735.

The first and most general division in the *Clavis Systematis Sexualis* rests upon the visibility of the sexual organs of the plant. Either the two sexes are visible and their marriages are public, or the two sexes are hidden, and their marriages are clandestine. The first of these considerations comprehends twenty-three classes based upon one of four dimensions: number, proportion, affinity, and situation. Number, the first attribute, comprehends the first eleven classes, the *Monandria, Diandria, Triandria, . . ., Decandria,* and *Dodecandria.* The twelfth class, or *Icosandria,* is based upon

16. Ibid., p. 174.
17. Lindman, p. 17.
18. *Ungdomsskrifter*, pp. 211, 279.
19. *Vita,* p. 139.
20. *Vita,* p. 138.

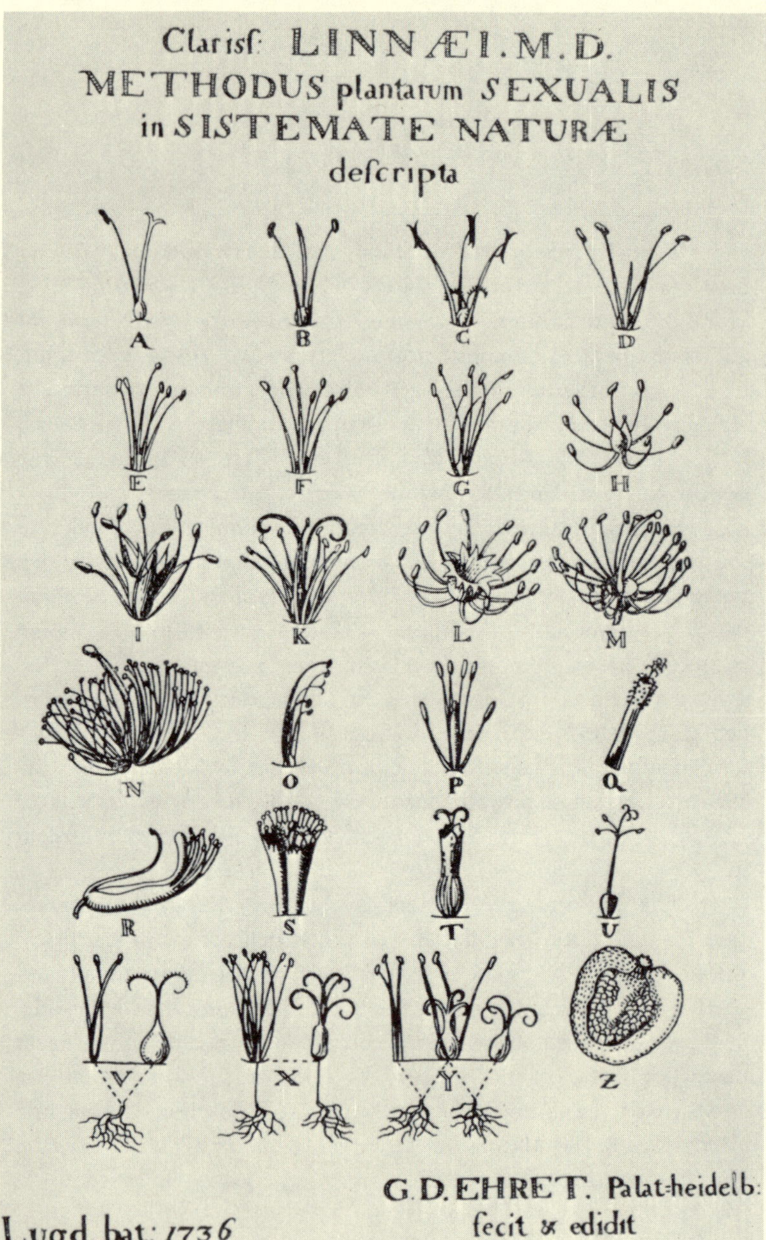

The classes of Linné's sexual system of classification as illustrated in Ehret's plate, 1736.

the insertion of the stamens on the calyx, while the thirteenth, or *Polyandria,* is based upon the insertion of the stamens upon the receptacle. The fourteenth and fifteenth classes, the *Didynamia* and the *Tetradynamia,* are based upon the proportion of the stamens, the *Didynamia* having two longer stamens and two shorter, the *Tetradynamia* having four longer stamens and two shorter. Four classes, the *Monadelphia, Diadelphia, Polyadelphia,* and the *Syngenesia,* are based upon the assemblage of filaments in one, two, or three bundles, and the anthers in one bundle. The twentieth class, or *Gynandria,* mentions stamens inserted on the pistil. The situation of the two sexual organs in distinct flowers on the same or different plants, and the mixture of these flowers with hermaphrodites provides means for forming three more classes, the *Monoecia, Dioecia,* and *Polygamia.* Finally, in his twenty-fourth class, the *Cryptogamia,* Linné assembled plants in which the fructification is hidden or unknown.

Linné divided these classes into orders on the following principles: in the first thirteen classes, founded upon stamen number, the orders were determined by the number of pistils: *Monogynia,* or one pistil, *Digynia,* two pistils, and so on, up to and including *Dodecagynia,* from eleven to twenty pistils, and *Polygynia,* twenty or more pistils. The fourteenth class, or *Didynamia,* contains two orders, the *Gymnospermia,* which includes plants with four naked seeds at the bottom of the calyx, and the *Angiospermia,* plants with seeds enclosed in a pericarp. The fifteenth class, or *Tetradynamia,* contains two orders, the *Siliculosa,* the fruit of which is a small pod or bivalve pericarp, and the *Siliquosa,* whose fruit is a genuine pod, that is, a bivalve pericarp four times as long as it is wide. In the *Monadelphia, Diadelphia, Polyadelphia, Gynandria, Monoecia,* and *Dioecia,* all based upon the adherence of filaments among themselves, with the ovary, or upon their position in various flowers, the orders were taken from the number of stamens, and the orders bear the names of the first classes, for example, *Monadelphia Pentandria, Polyadelphia Polyandria, Gynandria Diandria, Dioecia Diandria,* etc. The orders of the *Syngenesia* were based upon the disposition of two sexes and upon the disposition of flowers. This class was first divided in two orders, the *Syngenesia Polygamia,* in which several flowers are joined together in a common calyx, and the *Syngenesia Monogamia,* in which the flowers are separated.

The *Syngenesia Polygamia* were then divided in five orders, namely, the *Polygamia AEqualis,* in which all the flowers are hermaphrodites; the *Polygamia Superflua,* in which the central flowers are hermaphrodite, the marginal flowers female; the *Polygamia Frustranea,* in which the central flowers are hermaphrodite, the marginal sterile; the *Polygamia Necessaria,* in which only the marginal flowers are fertile; and finally, the *Polygamia Segregata,* in which the flowers, although enclosed in an involucrum, or common calyx, have each their own calyx. The twenty-third class, or the *Polygamia,* was divided in three orders based upon the distribution of three sorts of flowers, the *Polygamia Monoecia,* on one plant, the *Polygamia Dioecia,* upon two different individual plants, and the *Polygamia Trioecia,* upon three individual plants. Finally, the *Cryptogamia* were divided into four orders, the *Filices, Musci, Algæ,* and *Fungi.* These orders were simply taken from the general appearance of the plant and were not defined rigorously.[21]

The customary reference to the Linnæan system as a basically simple but ingenious arithmetical system founded upon the number of stamens and pistils, is, in fact, misleading. The principal divisions originate in the same four fundamental dimensions which afford the definitive marks for genera and species, namely, number, shape, proportion, and situation. Absolute number is only one among four of Linné's considerations.

The metaphorical language of the *Clavis Systematis Sexualis,* which betrays its origin in the plant-animal analogy, seems at first to have obscured somewhat the scientific content. Johann G. Siegesbeck attacked the system in 1737 on the grounds that God would not have allowed such shameless whoredom. What man would believe, inquired Siegesbeck, that God would introduce such harlotry into the propagation of the plant kingdom? Who would instruct youth in so voluptuous a system without scandal?[22] Linné, who always showed himself impatient of contradiction or of criticism, reacted violently. Responsible naturalists such as Amman

---

21. *Systema naturæ* (1735), unpaginated, 6th and 8th pages.
22. *Epicrisis in clarissimi Linnæi systema Plantarum sexuale* (1734). See also *Vaniloquentiæ Botanicæ specimen* (1741). Siegesbeck's attack has been described by W. T. Stearn in "An Introduction to the Species Plantarum and the Cognate Botanical Works of Carl Linnæus," *Species plantarum,* A Facsimile of the First Edition of 1753, vol. 1 (1957), p. 25.

who had jested rashly about Linné's "exceedingly odd" method felt obliged to reassure Linné that his scientific intention was clear.

> I could not suppose you would seriously be displeased at my remarking the great concourse of husbands to one wife, which often happens, and which is so unsuitable to the laws and manners of our people here. I was not speaking of those natural laws of the vegetable kingdom instituted by the Creator of all things.[23]

Professional botanical opinion came to Linné's support only toward the end of the decade. In 1739 Bernard de Jussieu, universally respected as an "oracle en fait d'histoire naturelle," pronounced the Linnæan method preferable to that of Tournefort because it was more exact.[24] Adrian van Royen in the preface to his *Floræ Leydensis* proclaimed Linné prince of botanists on the basis of the classification according to stamens and pistils. The system, said van Royen, had reformed the whole of botany, diffused fresh light over all its parts, and purged the science of its impurities.[25] Once professional opinion had directed itself upon Linné's scientific intention, discussion of the decency of Linné's metaphor lapsed.

French naturalists often alleged that the sexual system of classification admitted groupings and separations contrary to nature. Buffon, for example, complained that in emphasizing stamens alone, Linné, for the sake of his system, had forced nature to the point of confounding the most various objects, assembling

> le mûrier et l'ortie, la tulipe et l'épine-vinette, l'orme et la carotte, la rose et la fraise, le chêne et la pimprenelle.[26]

Adanson considered only the *Tetradynamia* and the *Monadelphia* among classes, and about one-fifth of Linné's orders, "natural."[27]

23. J. E. Smith, *A Selection of the Correspondence of Linnæus and Other Naturalists*, vol. 2 (1821), p. 193.
24. Bernard de Jussieu, "Histoire d'une Plante connue par les Botanistes sous le nom de Pilularia," *Mémoires de l'Académie des Sciences* (1739), pp. 244, 251.
25. Adrian van Royen, *Floræ Leydensis prodromus* (1734), p. 16.
26. Georges Louis de Buffon, "De la manière d'étudier et de traiter l'Histoire Naturelle," *Histoire naturelle générale et particulière* (1749), p. 18.
27. Michel Adanson, *Familles des Plantes*, Pt. I (1763), Préface, p. xl.

Antoine-Laurent de Jussieu complained that Linné, to retain the few groups which were justified by nature, had adopted characters rather unimportant and quite variable, and that his classes presented groupings inadmissible by a true naturalist.[28] It is true that Linné claimed to preserve as many natural classes with his classification as did any other method, but such preservation was not the primary aim of that classification.[29]

Linné intended his classification as a practical means of access to the well-established but numerous genera. The stamens and pistils are similar parts, readily characterized, easily seen, fairly constant in given kinds, yet varying sufficiently when viewed from their various aspects to operate a general division of the plant kingdom and to render the determination of genera easy and sure.

Linné discovered a more serious technical objection to his system in the variations among stamens in different species of one genus. In the *Valeriana (Triandria Monogynia),* for example, Linné noted a wonderful diversity in the number and figure of the different species. In most there were three stamens; in some two; in others one; in the Siberian species four; in others, the sexes were distinct.[30] Similar anomalies among the *Phytolacca, Geranium, Cleome, Polygonum,* and *Tillæa* were discovered subsequently.[31] In such cases Linné placed the genus in a class which indicated either the most common species, or the greatest number of species. At times flowers of the same plant exhibit a different number of stamens at different periods of growth. Linné placed the *Ruta* among the *Decandria* because the first flower had ten stamens, while the rest had eight.[32] Similar anomalies are found in the *Chrysoplenium, Adoxa,* etc.;[33] the difficulty of classification increases

28. Antoine-Laurent de Jussieu, *Genera plantarum* (1789), p. xxxiij. As examples of faulty grouping Jussieu cites the following: "in Diandriâ Piper et Jasminum, in Triandriâ Tamarindum et Iridem, in Tetrandriâ Rubiam et Evonymum, in Pentandriâ Primulam et Coffeam, Ulmum et Cicutam, in Hexandriâ Berberidem et Hyacinthum, in Octandriâ Tropæolum et Ericam, in Decandriâ Malpighiam et Alsinem, in Polyandriâ Chelidonium et Tiliam." A similar observation is found in a letter from Amman dated November 15, 1737; see Smith, vol. 2, p. 193.
29. *Classes plantarum,* p. xxxij.
30. *Genera plantarum* (1737), p. 8. See also *Genera plantarum* (1764), p. 22.
31. *Genera plantarum* (1764), pp. 233, 350, 345, 195, 126, 232, 68.
32. Ibid., p. 102.
33. Ibid., pp. 222, 198.

when the variation observes no fixed rule; Linné placed the *Trientalis,* for example, among the *Heptandria Monogynia,* and noted that the flower very much varied in number.[34] Variations were discovered in the female organs as well. At times plants were ordered according to the number of ovaries. The genera *Periploca, Cynanchum,* and *Asclepias,* all of which have two ovaries and one stylus, were placed in the *Pentandria Digynia,*[35] while the *Echites* and *Tabernæmontana,* which shared the same organization, were classed among the *Pentandria Monogynia.*[36]

Artificial systems were subject to such variations, and in working out his system, Linné catalogued such as did occur with increasing thoroughness. Yet these anomalies impaired the uniformity, universality, and facility which were the advantages of an artificial system. Other flaws were discovered subsequently. The genera classed under *Pentandria* proved to be so numerous that they were difficult to recognize. The orders of *Syngenesia* were founded on characters so minute, "il faut aller la microscope à la main," in Buffon's malicious expression, "pour reconnoître une plante."[37]

Flawed as it was, however, the scientific value of this artificial system seemed incontestable to Linné. The sense which Linné attributed to the artificiality of his system is best understood by contrasting the term with other characteristic expressions. The sexual system of classification was artificial, yet neither "arbitrary," nor "heterodox." An "arbitrary" system ramified at will in more extensive or abbreviated subdivisions from one section to another.[38] A well-defined system, which seemed to Linné infinitely preferable, consisted of five members appropriated to itself: class, order, genus, species, and variety. Such a system, because it did not fluctuate capriciously, guided and supported the mind by providing a palpable, regular sequence of signs. At the same time, the artificial system was "orthodox." Heterodox systems ranged plants alphabetically, or according to roots, leaves, habit, time of flowering, place of growth—in any case breaking up well-founded genera. Orthodox

34. Ibid., p. 183.
35. Ibid., pp. 119–120.
36. Ibid., pp. 118, 117.
37. Buffon, p. 19.
38. *Philosophia botanica,* § 154, p. 98.

systems, among which Linné reckoned his own, respected "natural" genera. The combinations of genera which resulted from classification according to the "most essential" parts of the plant were "artificial," but the simple elements of these combinations, the genera, remained "natural."[39] And even here the artificiality was not unmitigated. The characters of classes and orders were drawn from those same parts, the parts of fructification, which served to establish the genera.[40] Classification at every level proceeded according to fruit or flower considered under one of their universal dimensions, and in Linné's theory, naturalists, in classifying according to fructification, approached the activity inseparable from the "essence" of the plant.[41]

Nevertheless, Linné always considered his sexual system of classification a succedaneum for the natural method.[42] By forming classes and orders on the sexual organs of plants, the naturalist founded his system upon an essential set of characters, but in choosing a single part to determine all groups at one level, and in using that part exclusively, the sexual system of classification remained artificial.

Linné's reflections on the natural method form, therefore, a complement to his sexual system of classification. Aware to the difference between a practically commodious system and a method consonant with affinities observable in nature, Linné conceived a natural method which would represent all natural affinities fundamental in botany. All knowledge of natural objects depended upon the distinction of like from unlike. Such knowledge was, therefore, in proportion to the number of "real" or "natural" distinctions encompassed. The greater the number of distinctions a method could comprehend, the clearer became the ideas of natural objects. It was apparent as well, that the greater the number of objects upon which attention was directed, the more difficult it became to form such a method—and the more necessary.

39. Ibid., §§ 26–31, 53, pp. 12–13, 18.
40. Ibid., § 165, p. 116.
41. Ibid., § 88, pp. 56–57.
42. In a letter to Haller in 1737 Linné protests that he has never spoken of his "harmless sexual system" as a natural method (Smith, p. 232).

Linné first published his *Fragmenta Methodi Naturalis* in *Classes plantarum* in 1738.[43] This list contained sixty-five unnamed and uncharacterized orders under which genera were unevenly disposed. He published a revised list in 1751 in *Philosophia botanica,* the groups, or orders, designated with names derived from plant habit.[44] Linné presented his final views on the natural method in two courses of summer lectures, the first in 1764, the second in 1771. Giseke, on the basis of his own notes and those of Fabricius, published these lectures in 1792.[45] These lectures, with their amplifications and explanations, their complicated charts and genealogical maps, assemble most of Linné's later reflections on this involved subject. His earlier views, less explicit and more traditional, must be gleaned from stray remarks in the *Philosophia botanica* and from comment scattered up and down the pages of various editions of *Genera plantarum* and *Systema naturæ.*

The establishment of these "natural" groups represents in many ways a break with the thought which underlay the sexual system of classification. Linné's reflections on these groups, however, are extensions of the premises of his sexual system. This curious contrast between constitution and justification seems to explain Linné's admitted inability to achieve the natural method.

The groups listed in the *Fragmenta Methodi Naturalis* are based, not upon the reproductive function, but upon the general outward appearance of plants, or the so-called "*habitus.*"[46] Using such general resemblances, plants could be grouped, as Linné admitted, without injustice to actual, observable affinities.[47] The great danger in the use of plant habit was the vagueness about circumstances from which resemblances arose. Two organizations at bottom quite different might present a similar appearance, and conversely, a dissimilar appearance might mask a fundamental similarity. Procedures based upon plant habit often resulted in the constitution of erroneous or "unphilosophical" groups.

43. *Classes plantarum,* pp. 484–514.
44. *Philosophia botanica,* § 77, pp. 27–36.
45. *Prælectiones in ordines naturales plantarum* (1792).
46. *Philosophia botanica,* § 163, p. 101.
47. Ibid., p. 101.

Linné's attitude toward the use of plant habit was ambiguous. He was aware of its dangers; on the other hand, he found it advisable in practice to recur to a certain general coincidence of habit before defining and grouping plants officially.[48] Linné's remarks on the use of plant habit in establishing genera are illuminating. He admitted that an experienced botanist can readily determine from the habit of plants the family to which they belong, and that in this way the habit of plants serves as a check against establishing erroneous groupings. He cited as examples the *Nigella, Helleborus,* and *Caltha,* which are known to differ at first sight, and their difference is further confirmed by an examination of the fructification.[49] But the intuitive use of habit must remain a secondary procedure; however closely considered, no mark from a plant habit is ever to be used as a distinguishing factor.[50] In another place Linné pronounced an adherence to plant habit for the characters of plants "great folly"; fructification is judged "the only true principle of systematic arrangement."[51] In short, plant habit was indispensable in the constitution of genera, but it was only to be represented as a secondary guide owing to its want of exactness.

This same line of thought pervades Linné's presentation of the natural orders. Higher groups may be established intuitively on the basis of plant habit, but they are to be defined on the basis of fructification. In the *Philosophia botanica* Linné admitted that the natural method is in great measure based upon habit, and that fructification is not yet so thoroughly understood as to discover all the classes of the natural method, though it may be considered as the primary guide to them.[52] Linné immediately qualified this admission, however, with the principle, that the primary disposition, or arrangement of plants, ought to be derived from the parts of fructification only.[53] Giseke reports a conversation

---

48. According to one of his most virulent critics, F. K. Medicus, Linné's use of plant habit was far more fundamental that Linné admitted. See W. T. Stearn, "Notes on Linnæus's 'Genera Plantarum,'" *Three Prefaces on Linnæus and Robert Brown* (1962), p. xii.

49. *Philosophia botanica,* § 208, p. 138. See also § 205, p. 136.

50. Ibid., § 168, p. 117.

51. Ibid., § 209, pp. 139–140.

52. Ibid., § 163, p. 101.

53. Ibid., § 164, p. 112.

some twenty years later which contained similar ideas. Linné had asked Giseke for the distinctive character of the *Umbellatæ*. Giseke replied that they were plants in which the flowers were disposed in an umbel. Linné agreed, but reminded Giseke that plants other than the *Umbellatæ* form umbels. Giseke then added two bare seeds to his characteristic marks. Then, asked Linné, do you exclude the *Echinophera?* In other words, groups based upon plant habit remained vague, unverifiable, and subject to exception.[54] A classification based upon habit was therefore unscientific. On the other hand, unexceptionable characters were not to be found in the parts of fructification. General resemblances might indicate a fundamental similarity, but Linné could discover no way of confirming this similarity in the parts of fructification. Linné's limitation of definitive characters to the parts of fructification made it impossible for him to discover any relation among genera less artificial than his system based upon stamens and pistils, for once above the level of genera, the representation of affinities rests, as later naturalists demonstrated, upon a subtle conception of the whole of plant structure.

Linné defined orders as genera of genera,[55] and classes as genera of orders,[56] or as assemblages of several genera agreeing in the parts of fructification.[57] The classic character, taken from the parts of fructification, comprehended the "essential" determination in which all subordinate genera agreed, each genus in turn defined by a character belonging only to that genus. On the other hand, Linné was confronted with a collection of well-established "natural" groups, such as the *Umbellatæ,* for which he was unable to find definitive characters in the parts of fructification. He spoke of these groups as "natural orders,"[58] and showed how these orders might be combined in even more basic groups, the chief of which were based upon the disposition of the lobes of the seed at the time when the seed begins to sprout.[59]

54. *Prælectiones*, p. xvii.
55. *Critica Botanica*, § 251, p. 108.
56. Ibid., § 251, p. 108.
57. *Philosophia botanica*, § 160, p. 100.
58. Ibid., p. 100.
59. Ibid., § 163, p. 102. See § 78, p. 37, for a division of plants into seven families on the basis of increasing complexity.

Linné's thought here issues from the same source which led him to select the stamens and pistils as the most essential parts of the flower. The aim of the sexual function is reproduction. The stamens and pistils are means to this end. The seed, or rather, the embryonic plant contained in this seed must, then, be considered the most essential part of the reproductive system because it is the aim of the entire process of generation. This embryonic plant must furnish characters for the first division of plants since it is a distinct individual in which are concentrated all of the differences which will influence its general development and structure. The first discoverable differences in this embryonic plant consist in the number of lobes or cotyledons. Hence there arises a tripartite division of plants: *dicotyledons,* that is, plants having two lobes, *monocotyledons,* or plants having one lobe, and *acotyledons,* plants having no lobes. This division seemed justified, not simply because it rested upon the assemblage of all plant characters *in nuce,* but also because it preserved all "natural" orders and most well-established genera.[60] But this division had one flaw. The "natural orders" were established only upon the basis of plant habit, and the cotyledons were an element, not of fructification, but of vegetation. The use of the cotyledons as a basis for classification was insecure; the resulting groups were incorrectly established. The problem was how to ascertain, determine, and reconstitute these natural groups on the basis of fructification.

Linné's contributions to subsequent thought about the natural method lay in his attempt to reconcile acknowledged "natural" groups with his scientific preoccupations. The first of these contributions was the principle that there are no a priori rules for constituting plant groups from the parts of fructification.[61] This principle seems to have arisen from Linné's experience in two areas: the application of his artificial system of classification, and the formation of genera. The "artificiality" of the sexual system of classification lay in grouping plants by means of a single character applied exclusively. This application led to groupings and separations contrary to "nature." At the same time Linné's experience

60. *Præludia sponsaliorum plantarum,* § XXVIII, p. 19; *Classes plantarum,* p. 487; *Systema naturæ* (1735), unpaginated, 9th page, No. 6; *Philosophia botanica,* §§ 88, 163, pp. 56–57, 102; *Prælectiones,* pp. xix–xx.
61. *Classes plantarum,* p. 487.

of genera had shown that plants which agreed in some part of fructification, or in some dimension of the parts of fructification, were nevertheless distinct genera. There was no way to determine what was constant in all the species of a genus but examination and observation. Such examination showed that some parts or dimensions were more constant than others.

For example, the number of parts in a flower varied more greatly than the figure, while the relative position of parts was, in general, the most constant of all possible dimensions.[62] But this constancy, though it held in most instances, could not be depended upon, since there were no perfectly constant characters.[63] The characters which served to establish one genus did not necessarily have the same constitutive value for another genus.[64] Linné extended this experience in the constitution of genera to cover the constitution of natural classes and orders. No system founded upon the examination of a single part, whatever that part might be, could include all plants, since no single part was found in every plant. This generalization, confirmed by Adanson's work in artificial systems published in 1763, mitigated the speculative rigor of strict adherence to fructification, and led to an examination by later naturalists of all possible factors, affinities, and relations in play among parts.

The second of Linné's contributions to subsequent thought about the natural method was his principle of symmetry. No a priori rule could be admitted in a natural method and no part of fructification could be considered exclusively; the naturalist, therefore, had to consider the symmetry of all parts *(symmetria omnium partium)*.[65] The idea of plant symmetry, a whole resulting from the relative disposition of interacting parts, seems to have been a recognition by Linné that the function and importance of individual parts is modified by the general plan or organization in a plant. This idea became important after Antoine-Laurent de Jussieu had demonstrated associations of characters of greater or lesser variability. Augustin-Pyrame de Candolle took up Linné's principle of symmetry in his theory of natural classification and

62. *Philosophia botanica*, §§ 178,179, pp. 123–124.
63. Ibid., § 175, p. 123.
64. Ibid., § 175, p. 123.
65. *Classes plantarum*, p. 487.

developed a subtle analysis of plant abortions, multiplications, degenerations, and adherences based upon relative disposition and the general tendency of plants toward symmetrical wholes.[66]

Linné's final reflections upon the natural method contained new impulses which resulted from his attempt to resolve problems issuing from his early belief in the fixity of species. These problems forced Linné to reevaluate temporal factors in natural history. As assumptions about continuity of form merged with the notion of community of origin, Linné sought to locate the process of group creation in the break up of the higher taxa. Adhering to Aristotle's idea that the fructification is part of the medulla descending from the mother, and that vegetation is part of the cortex descending from the father, Linné concluded that plants which have arisen from a mixture of two different plants are similar to the mother in fructification and belong, as her daughters, to her group, although they resemble the father in general appearance.[67]

In this amalgam of ideas, the limitation of parts to two exclusive functional systems, the preeminence accorded fructification, even the causal explanations were old; only the stress on the creative element of time was new. This element became increasingly important in Linné's thought, and with its increasing emphasis, Linné tended to extend its influence to the class hierarchy. In the *Fundamenta fructificationis* Linné imagined that God had created one species for each natural order of plants which differs in habit and fructification from all others. These species, mutually fertile, gave birth to as many genera as there were different parents, their fructification somewhat changed. Linné regarded this generic creation as supernatural as well. All genera were primeval and consisted originally of one species. In the course of time these genera were fertilized and produced as many species as then existed; these species, fertilized in turn, produced varieties.[68] In the *Prælectiones* Linné advanced supernatural creation one step higher and brought genera into the order of time.

> The principle being accepted that all species of one genus have arisen from one mother through different fathers, it must be assumed:

66. De Candolle, *Théorie élémentaire de la Botanique* (1804), pp. 72–123.
67. *Philosophia botanica*, § 78, p. 37.
68. *A.A.*, vol. 6, pp. 300–301.

1) That in the beginning the Creator created of each natural order only one plant with reproductive power.

2) That by their various mixings different plants have arisen which belong to the mother's natural order as they are similar to the mother with regard to their fructifications, and are, as it were, species of the order, i.e. genera.

3) We may assume that plants have arisen within the orders, i.e. by genera of one order, may mix with each other. In this way there will arise species that should be referred to the mother's genus as her daughters.[69]

It is characteristic of Linné, however, and of natural history of his period, that he should represent these temporal relations, not as a genealogical table, but as a genealogical-geographical map, and that the tissue of relations should seem to him to reconcile the natural method with the Aristotelian principle of continuity. The image of plant affinities as a geographical map first appeared in *Philosophia botanica* after the traditional assertion of the principle of continuity.[70] The traditional image of plant continuity was that of an unbroken chain in which each link was a species contiguous to two other species, forming a single line. But Linné considered the principal features of natural relations to be the resemblances among plant clusters which permitted them to be classified in distinct groups. These groups were in turn disposed in larger groups; the plant kingdom was at last a very large group containing a mass of inferior groups. This order was best represented, not as a chain with each link in contact with two other links, but as a geographical map in which each territory formed a center which corresponded with several surrounding points.[71]

This image must have been constantly in Linné's mind during his final lectures on the subject of the natural method, for one of his chief concerns throughout is a survey of connections between genera and between natural orders.[72] The noted likenesses extend not only to preceding or succeeding plant groups, but in many directions, and comprehend not only fructification, but vegetation as well. The rigidity of the traditional linear image is softened.

69. *Prælectiones*, pp. 16, 18.
70. *Philosophia botanica*, § 77, p. 27.
71. *Prælectiones*, pp. 2, 623–627.
72. Ibid.; see the discussions of *Piperitæ, Orontium, Acorus,* etc.

The image of a geographical map was taken up subsequently by Antoine-Laurent de Jussieu, Bernardin de Saint Pierre, L'Heritier, Petit Thouars, and de Candolle. It was found to be so apt and so fertile in useful suggestions as to be an adequate representation of natural relations.

The elements of Linné's thought about natural method which found the greatest response among naturalists during the second half of the eighteenth century tended to mitigate the stringency of tradition. Linné's principle that there are no a priori rules ended the dominion of speculative physiology, and encouraged a renewed examination of all possible resemblances. Linné's principle of symmetry led to a new conception of the wholes and the parts of plants founded upon a more careful examination of structure, accommodating the rationale of plant monstrosities, deviations, and anomalies. The image of a geographical map to represent plant relations suggested a more intimate and a more accurate conception of the multiple affinities which held between plants.

Linné's admitted failure to achieve a natural method seems, however, to stem, at least in part, from his inability to break out of the perspective imposed by tradition and to make the implications of his insights somewhat more explicit. Accustomed to find the most essential parts of plants in the system of fructification, Linné tended to neglect the system of vegetation and the diverse points of view from which it might be considered.

Linné offered two practical reasons for his failure to achieve the natural method: (1) the want of genera, particularly tropical genera, and (2) an inability to discover definitive characters in the parts of fructification. Linné's reasoning about lacunae in tropical genera is readily explained. A "natural" grouping required the examination of all members in order to note all pertinent affinities. This condition could not be met as long as tropical genera were not fitted in among the genera already known. There were, in other words, unexplored territories on the genealogical map.[73]

The second reason which Linné offered for his failure to achieve the natural method, an inability to discover definitive characters in the system of fructification, reveals, however, a fundamental flaw in the organization of his enterprise. For from Linné's

73. *Philosophia botanica*, e.g., §§ 77, 160, 206, 208, 209, pp. 27, 100, 137, 138, 139.

remarks it is clear that he attributed his failure to find such definitive characters to inadequate knowledge. In the *Philosophia botanica,* for example, he stated that fructification is not sufficiently understood to reveal the classes of the natural method.[74] Linné in his later statements was a good deal more pessimistic, but he never abandoned completely the idea that definitive characters for natural orders are to be sought in the reproductive system. In the *Prælectiones* Linné said that characters for the natural orders will be needed to develop the natural method in botany, but that discovering such characters is impossible.[75] In one of his autobiographies Linné even went so far as to say that the key to the natural orders will not be found before the *quadratura circuli* is hit upon. Yet, in the same sentence, Linné speaks of his contributions toward the natural method as his masterpiece.

> In this Linné himself set his masterpiece. Many have tried to refine it, but all to no avail. He who can give the key to this has found *methodus naturalem,* but [that] shouldn't happen before *quadratura circuli* is hit upon; he who uses it instead of method is building a house without a roof. D. Jussieu liked this best, read and persuaded his pupils of it, and gave it out for method; it is matchless for *natura plantæ,* but without definition it is a bell without a clapper. Many have thought they had defined it when they had given *notas communes,* but no one has given such as separate one order from other orders. He who understands *fundamentum fructificationis et species hybridas ex generatione ambigena* understands why it is impossible.[76]

One can understand this impasse only by surveying Linné's assumptions about the constitution and justification of plant groups. The continuity of theory from the *Præludia,* written in 1729, through the *Clavis Systematis Sexualis,* published in 1735, to the *Prælectiones,* delivered in 1764 and 1771, consists in this, that the "essentiality" of the system of fructification and its preeminence as an instrument of classification is never questioned.

In characteristically vehement expressions, Linné repeatedly identified fructification as a system, the physiological activity of

---

74. Ibid., § 168, p. 117.
75. *Prælectiones,* p. xvii.
76. *Vita,* p. 170.

which is inseparable from the "essence" of plants, and the use of the parts of fructification as the only true principle of systematic arrangement. At the same time Linné seemed always to have had in mind the general appearance or habit of plants which he used to establish plant groups justified subsequently on the basis of fructification. Linné's attitude toward plant habit as a basis of classification arises from the vagueness with which resemblances are described; groups founded upon plant habit often contain exceptions, and, owing to a want of phytographical exactness, resemblances are unverifiable. This explains, at least partially, why Linné wished to establish the higher groups in his natural method on the basis of fructification, even after he had composed these groups with great perspicuity on the basis of general resemblance.

The actual constitution of Linné's natural orders breaks, then, with the theoretical justification which Linné offers for the artificial sexual system of classification and the determination of genera. The attempted justification of these natural orders, on the other hand, is only a generalization of Linné's experience of genera and of artificial systems. For these reasons the fragments of Linné's natural method are juxtaposed, as Daudin points out, with a practical systematic construction, but are never quite integrated in that construction. In other words, the orientation of Linné's theory was constant, but the relative importance of the aspects of plant forms upon which that theory was directed differed.[77] This seems to account for the conflict between intuition and justification found in Linné's contributions toward the natural method.

The problem of classes and orders in Linnæan systematic thought remained unsolved. Practical disposition and natural affinities were never resolved at the higher levels of the Linnæan system. The artificial sexual system of classification, which satisfied limited professional requirements, could not attain any significant contact with knowledge of natural objects. At the highest levels, at least, the natural method could not be established satisfactorily. Linné's arbitrary limitation of definitive characters to the parts of fructification made it impossible for him to discover any grouping of genera less artificial than the system of classification based upon stamens and pistils.

77. Daudin, *De Linné à Jussieu*, p. 43.

Chapter III

GENERA

Although Linné failed to work out "natural" classes and orders, he considered all genera "natural," "the work of nature," and the foundation of theoretical botany.[1] The artificial sexual system, far from rendering subsumed genera suspect or provisory, was justified in theory because it respected natural genera, and in practice because it provided easy access to the solidly established genera. Equally, a natural method was to be justified, not because it would fix the genera once and for all—Linné regarded the genera as fixed already—but because relations above the level of genera would be as well founded as the genera themselves.

The concept of the genus, however, presented difficulties. There were two extremes to be avoided: the use of minute distinctions resulting in an unnecessary multiplication of genera, and the use of gross distinctions resulting in the confusion of genera. As an example of too minute distinctions Linné cites *Cardiaca* established by Tournefort on the basis of a five-toothed calyx. Linné says that if genera were multipled in this manner without any necessity, there would be as many genera as species.[2] As an example of inadequate distinctions Linné cites the incorporation of *Androm-eda* and *Erica*; the *Erica* had subsequently to be separated from

1. *Philosophia botanica*, §§ 162, 209, pp. 101, 139. *General plantarum* (1737), "Ratio opera," unpaginated, second, third, and fourth pages, nos. 6, 10. *Systema Naturæ* (1735), unpaginated, ninth page, no. 14. See also J. A. Nannfeldt, "Presidential Address," *Systematics of to-day* (1958), p. 7.
2. *Philosophia botanica*, § 170, p. 121.

73

the *Andromeda* because of two more conspicuous horns on the anthers in *Erica*.[3]

Besides the problem of adequate distinctions, there was that of artificiality. Unlike the artificial classes and orders of the sexual system, genera could not be established upon a single part. In some genera, Linné observes, one part, in other genera another part, is more constant than the rest, but none of them is perfectly constant *(constantissima)*.[4]

In short, Linné's concern in establishing genera was to find characters of appreciably equal value without settling upon single characters applied exclusively.

An appeal to general appearance was fundamental to Linné's establishment of genera. Not only did plant habit serve as a check against constituting erroneous genera;[5] characters taken from plant habit served to establish plant groupings intuitively. Before Linné fixed upon the technical characters which defined plants as one genus, he invoked a coincidence of general appearance. In a letter to Abraham Bäck, the younger Linné describes his father's practice in constituting genera.

> My blessed father's secret of determining, so that species did not become genera, was nothing more than the habit of knowing the outward appearance of the plant; therefore he often departed from his own method so that variation in the number of parts did not disturb him if the character of the genus could still be retained; . . .If [it were] possible he tried to ground the generic character on the partition of the fruit, so that all the species which constituted a genus had the same form of fruit.[6]

This is the sense, too, of Linné's principle, *Characterem non constituero Genus, sed Genus Characterem*.[7] Unlike the higher classes of the sexual system of classification, the genera were not to be established on the appreciation of a single character. Plants were

3. Ibid., § 172, p. 122.
4. Ibid., § 175, p. 123.
5. Ibid., § 168, pp. 117–118.
6. Arvid Hjalmar Uggla, "Linné den yngres brev till Abraham Bäck 1778," *Svenska Linné-Sällskapets Årsskrift*, Årg. XXXIX–XL (1957), p. 150.
7. *Philosophia botanica*, § 169, p. 119.

to be grouped provisorily on the basis of general resemblance, then confirmed as genera by nearer examination.

Characters taken from plant habit suffered, however, from a want of exactness. Such characters could not, therefore, afford distinctions of equal value. Genera established on this basis had to be rejected. The *Limodorum* and *Bistorta* of Tournefort, for example, established on varying root composition were relegated by Linné to the *Orchis* and *Polygonum* respectively.[8] In Linné's practice, consultation of plant habit was an indispensable guide to the constitution of genera; plant habit remained unmentioned, however, in the definition of genera for want of precision.

In Linné's opinion only the parts of fructification offered varying characters of appreciably equal value suitable to the constitution of genera. Plants agreeing in parts of fructification were, other things being equal, to be combined; all plants differing in parts of fructification were to be separated.[9] *Genera tot dicimus,* states Linné, *quot similes constructæ fructificationes proferunt diversæ species naturales.*[10]

Linné's reliance upon fructification is, as both Daudin and Stearn have pointed out, a dogmatization of the practice of Tournefort.[11] Before the time of Tournefort the concept of the genus had been very unstable.[12] Tournefort's great innovation was to limit the constitution of genera to purely botanical characters, and on this basis to fix and to characterize neighboring genera unequivocally.

> To have a clear idea of the word genus in the sense in which one ought to take it for botany, we must remark that it is absolutely necessary in this science, to bring together as in bouquets plants which resemble one another, and to separate them from those which they do not resemble. This resemblance should be drawn exclusively from their affinities, that is to say, from the structure of some of their parts;

8. Ibid., § 164, p. 114.
9. Ibid., §§ 165, 166, p. 116.
10. Ibid., § 159, p. 100.
11. Daudin, *De Linné à Jussieu* (1926), p. 36, and W. T. Stearn, "Notes on Linnæus's 'Genera Plantarum,'" in *Three Prefaces*, p. viii.
12. Dughi, "Tournefort dans l'histoire de la botanique," *Tournefort* (1957), pp. 156–161.

one need not pay attention to the distant relations between certain plants, as, for example, virtues they may have, or places where they grow. We shall consider plants amongst which the same structures of parts are found as plants within the same genus, in such a way that we shall call a genus of plants the sum of all those which share a common character that distinguishes them essentially from all others.[13]

In seeking these common characters Tournefort examined closely the five chief parts of the plant, root, stem, leaf, flower, and fruit. He concluded that flower and fruit were absolutely necessary for the establishment of all genera whose species bore fruit and flowers, but that these parts did not sufficiently distinguish all genera. Tournefort then applied this principle methodically, and offered for genus after genus discriminative characters, or combinations of characters, drawn from fruit and flower adequate to delimit and to stabilize even closely related groups or "bouquets" of species.

The limitation of generic characters to the parts of fructification, to fruit and flower, was an important step toward the stabilization of the concept of the botanical genus, and Tournefort's work served as a basis for the *Genera* of Linné (first edition, 1737) and of Antoine-Laurent de Jussieu (1789). In his *Genera* Linné acknowledges that Tournefort did wonders with his characters, but adds that since so many and such new genera have been discovered one should adhere to his principles, but augment them with new discoveries as the science increases.[14] Elsewhere Linné finds the parts described by Tournefort insufficient and asks why petals and fruit alone were acknowledged and whether there were not other equally necessary parts of fructification.[15]

Linné considers his own analysis of fructification and his subsequent constitution of genera on the basis of this analysis a sovereign discovery and his chief contribution to the fixation of genera. He conceives his analysis as a breakdown of a primal system of fructification into a small number of simple elements. These simple elements are the components of all fructification; the varied combinations of these simple elements obtain every possible dispo-

13. *Elemens de Botanique*, p. 13.
14. "Ratio operis," unpaginated, fifth page, no. 12.
15. Ibid., fifth page, no. 11.

sition of fructification, just as the combination of letters of the alphabet engenders a multitude of complex concepts.

> These marks are to us so many vegetable letters, which,
> if we can read, will teach us the characters of plants; they
> are written by the hand of God; it should be our study
> to read them.[16]

Since, in Linnæan theory, the "nature" and "essence" of a plant reside in the system and activity of fructification,[17] a vegetable alphabet based upon this system approaches the activity inseparable from the "nature" of the plant; in spelling out the various combinations of this alphabet, the naturalist obtains infallibly the definition of all genera.

Linné's analysis of these vegetable letters is, as Sachs admits, more thorough than that of Tournefort or indeed of any predecessor, but it reveals as well an "incapacity for the careful investigation of any object at all difficult to observe."[18] Fructification, which Linné defines as a temporary element in plants appointed for the purpose of terminating the old plant and beginning the new, is broken down into seven chief parts, beginning with the two floral envelopes, the calyx and the corolla.[19]

The calyx, or termination of the outer rind of the plant, includes seven kinds: the *perianthium,* or flower cup proper, the *involucrum,* or cover of the *Umbellifera,* the *amentum,* or catkin, consisting of a chaffy series of scales proceeding from a slender thread as in willows, the *spatha,* or sheath, bursting lengthways and putting forth a stalk as in the *Narcissus,* the *gluma,* or husk, peculiar to grasses, the *calyptra,* or hood, peculiar to mosses and resembling a monk's cowl, and the *volva,* peculiar to fungi and involving or enclosing their fructification. The corolla, or termina-

---

16. Ibid., fifth page, no. 11.
17. *Philosophia botanica,* § 88, p. 56.
18. *History of Botany* (1890), pp. 96–97.
19. The exposition here follows the order in the *Philosophia botanica,* §§ 86–114, pp. 52–75. The English is based upon a very unreliable translation by Hugh Rose, *The Elements of Botany* (1775). The best guide to eighteenth-century terminology is de Candolle's "Glossologie," *Théorie élémentaire de la Botanique* (1844), pp. 283–442. See also Termini botanici, *A.A.,* vol. 6, pp. 217–246.

tion of the inner rind of the plant, is further broken down into the petals and the nectarium. These two floral envelopes, the calyx and the corolla, which at first cover the sexual organs of plants, open, when the plant has reached a degree of maturity, and disclose the sexual organs—the stamens and the pistils. The female organ, or the pistil, occupies the center of the plant and consists of the *germen,* or seed bud, containing the rudiments of the unripe fruit in the flowering state of the plant, the *stigma,* and the *stylus,* respectively receiving the fertilizing dust and transmitting its effluvia to the seed bud. The pistil is surrounded by one or more male organs, or stamens, which elaborate the fecundating dust, and which consist of three parts, the *filament,* or support, the *anther,* or container of the *aura seminalis,* and the *pollen,* or impregnating dust proper. Under the influence of the vegetation and the action of the sun, the anthers open and discharge a fine powder upon the stigma. The stamens and the corolla, become useless, fall away, and the saps which they absorbed are diverted to the fertilized ovary.

Linné treated the ripening fruit, not as a developing ovary, but as a new part, the pericarp, which he defined as that part which contains the seeds and discharges them when ripe. Linné described eight kinds of pericarp, capsules, pods, cods, bags, stone fruits, apples, berries, and cones. Linné defined the discharged seed as that deciduous part of the plant which contains the rudiments of the new plant. In the seed proper Linné distinguished the following parts: the *corculum,* or little heart (on the analogy with the animal heart, first living part of the embryo), which in turn is composed of the *plumula* thrusting upward to become a stem, and the *rostellum* striking downward to become a root; the *cotyledon,* the porous, perishable side lobe of the seed; the *hilum,* an external cicatrix left by the seed attachment; the *arillus,* an outer coat which falls off spontaneously; the *coronula,* a seed crown either feathered or hairy; and finally, the *ala,* or seed wings, by means of which the seed is dispersed. Linné also relegated to the seed the nut with its characteristic osseous cover, and the *propago,* or seed of mosses, which has no covering. The seventh and final part of fructification is the *receptaculum,* by which Linné meant everything connecting the other six parts. This includes the *receptaculum proprium* uniting the parts of a single flower, and the *receptaculum commune,* which comprises quite various forms of inflorescence.

All plants perform a reproductive function by means of some combination of these fundamental elements. There are, in all, by Linné's calculation, some thirty-eight simple elements in the system of fructification.[20]

Each of these simple elements of fructification, described in turn from one of four aspects or dimensions, number, shape, proportion, and situation *(numerus, figura, proportio, situs)*, obtains the marks from which the definition or description of the genus is composed.[21] Linné's choice of dimensions for considering the simple elements of fructification reveals a curious but highly characteristic division between intrinsic and derivative determinations of natural objects. Time and space are frames of reference ordering natural objects; they affect natural objects, but the resultant determinations are derivative, extrinsic.[22] As for aspects of natural objects discovered by the senses, odor and savor are unusable because they vary with the observer, and hearing is indemonstrable.[23] Not even all qualities discovered by sight are reliable. Color, for example, is strangely sportive and therefore unreliable.[24] Size varies with situation;[25] a comparative size is unscientific because it makes one plant a standard for the study of another.[26] "What I like," says Linné, "are distinctions that are definite and capable of demonstration."[27] There are but four certain and fundamental distinctions, or universal dimensions, by which alone one plant's differences are represented to us, namely, number, shape, proportion, and situation. These are the dimensions represented in pictures and preserved in herbaria; these are the qualities which have real value; they lay the foundation of science like a rock, and, concluded Linné, *structa super lapidem, qui ruet ista domus?*[28]

---

20. *Philosophia botanica*, § 167, pp. 116–117.
21. Ibid., §§ 92, 167, 176, pp. 59, 116, 123.
22. In the *Critica botanica* Linné says, for example, that season of flowering is not imprinted on plants, so it ought not to be incorporated in the diagnostic phrase (§ 265, p. 136), and that locality makes plants a little different, but never changes one species into another (§ 264, p. 130).
23. Ibid., §§ 267, 268, pp. 142–145.
24. Ibid., § 266, pp. 138–142.
25. Ibid., § 260, pp. 123–125.
26. Ibid., § 260, p. 123.
27. Ibid., § 267, p. 144.
28. Ibid., § 282, p. 161.

Linné attributed great importance to number in parts, probably, as de Candolle suggests, because of its apparent exactness.[29] Emphasis upon absolute number in the sexual system of classification had revealed its instability, however, and in the *Philosophia botanica* Linné admitted that as a dimension number is more subject to variation than shape or situation, and that some elements of fructification vary more greatly in number than others.[30] In utilizing these discoveries Linné's treatment of absolute number concerns itself with showing how numerical variation can be related to the basic type of a group in order to discover plant genus. Linné noted, for example, that in polypetalous flowers, the lowest series of petals, remaining always the same in number, even in full flowers, reveals the genus,[31] and that the stamens and the calyx, being less liable to luxuriance, are more certain even than petals.[32]

The consideration of absolute number leads almost imperceptibly to a study of proportional number. Linné noted that in the "most natural" numerical relation, the calyx is divided into as many segments as the corolla; that the filaments are of the same number; that each filament is furnished with a single anther; and that the division of the pistil agrees with the cells of the seed vessel.[33] Again, in studying variations in these relations, Linné notes a proportional affinity: in flowers the stamens vary from eight to ten and from four to five; the corolla and calyx from five to four, and the whole flower from four to three; and finally, the fruit from five to three, and from five to four.[34]

Linné considered the dimension of number, then, under an absolute and a relative aspect. In both cases Linné was concerned with the extraction of differentiae suitable to the definition of plant groups. For this reason the regular and suggestive irregularities of the dimension of number were alluded to, but not systematized.

Under the dimension of shape, Linné included not only a great variety of plane and cubic forms, but also substances and textures, joints and terminations. Linné described the "most natu-

29. *Théorie élémentaire de la Botanique*, p. 131.
30. *Philosophia botanica*, § 178, p. 123.
31. Ibid., § 185, p. 128.
32. Ibid., § 182, p. 125.
33. Ibid., § 94, p. 60.
34. Ibid., § 178, pp. 123–124.

ral" shape of fructification as one in which the calyx is less spreading than the corolla, which in turn widens upward and is furnished within with filaments and pistils standing upright and tapering. When these parts (with the exception of the calyx) have fallen, the pericarp swells and continues to grow.[35] Again Linné noted greater and lesser variations in constancy among elements of fructification with respect to shape. The form of the flower, for example, is more constant than that of the fruit.[36] In distinguishing more exactly the variations in the shape of simple elements, Linné noted textures, consistencies, articulations, and terminations. He distinguished the calyx, for example, by overall shape (*cucubalus, clavatus, reflexus, erectus*), composition (*integerrimus, serratus, ciliatus*), and termination (*acutus, acuminatus, obtusus*).[37] The dimension of shape, in other words, lends itself to delicate and precise discriminations for which Linné discovered a large vocabulary in geometrical forms (*ellipsoideus, sphericus, globosus, linearis*), in metaphor (*echinatus, digitaliformis, carinatus*), and in visual and tactile qualities (*splendens, dura, exasperatus, glutinosus*).[38]

In Linné's opinion absolute size is unreliable. Whether a plant considered by itself is big or small, short or tall, matters little. Such size changes as outside influences change. Any change in situation or nourishment is apt to bring about a variation.

> All plants growing in barren exhausted dry soil are smaller,
> and become larger where it is spongy, moist, and fertile.
> . . . All plants in the alps are small, while outside that
> region they grow taller.[39]

The size of elements compared amongst themselves, however, remains constant in ratio, although the simple elements vary greatly. Therefore, according to Linné, proportion of parts is always most constant and definite.[40] Linné described the "most natural" proportion in fructification as one in which the calyx is smaller than the corolla and the stamens and pistils are of equal length with

---

35. Ibid., § 95, p. 60.
36. Ibid., § 177, p. 123.
37. Ibid., § 99, p. 63.
38. Ibid., § 95, p. 60.
39. *Critica botanica*, § 260, p. 123.
40. *Philosophia botanica*, § 177, p. 123.

the calyx—if the flower is erect.[41] The general discriminations of proportion in Linné's *Genera plantarum* are comparative, either with some normative expectation (as in *maxima, minima, major, minor*), or with another element of fructification either expressed or understood (as in *æqualis, inæqualis*). The more particular discriminations of proportion in the simple elements of fructification are relative to one of three dimensions: length (*longus, brevis, elongatus, abbreviatus*), breadth (*platys, angustus, extensus*), and thickness (*crassus, tenuis, æqualis*). There are in Linné's vocabulary some three-dimensional terms for proportion (*megalos, amplus, mediocris*), some of which are modified by form (*pygmæus, depressus, humilis, exaltatus*).

Situation, for Linné, was, however, the most constant of all dimensions, scarcely differing in plants of the same genus.[42] Linné described the "most natural" situation of fructification as one in which the perianth or the calyx surrounds the receptacle; the corolla is set upon the receptacle and alternates with the calyx; the filaments are situated within the corolla opposite its segments; the anthers are seated on the tops of the filaments; the germen occupies the center of the receptacle; the stylus stands on the top of the germen, and the stigma are seated on the top of the stylus. When these fall off, the germen grows to a seed vessel supported by the calyx and including within itself the seeds fixed to the receptacle of the fruit. In treating the variants of this "most natural" situation, Linné considers them in relation to immediate support, or to heterogeneous elements by which parts are surrounded. Under the rubric of situation, therefore, Linné included a large vocabulary for discriminations which concern, not only relative situation, but also direction (*verticalis, erectus, spiralis*), insertion (*dorsalis, lateralis, terminalis*), attachment (*cohærens, articulatis, pedunculatus*), and disposition (*stellatus, spiralis, verticillatus*).

Linné's analysis of fructification consisted, then, of two parts: an organography, and a characteristic. Linné's organography resolved the system of fructification into thirty-eight simple elements. These elements are the irreducible components in any "scientific" reconstitution of genera, an alphabet from which the more complex combinations of fructification must be spelled out. Each of these simple elements, or vegetable letters, may be viewed in turn from

41. Ibid., § 96, pp. 60–61.
42. Ibid., § 179, p. 124. See also *Classes plantarum*, p. 487.

four aspects, or dimensions, namely, number, shape, proportion, and situation, which afford intrinsic marks defining the genus. The system of fructification, focused upon well-defined visual and tactile shapes, brings the essential or definitive factors of the plant genus to mind. Linné concluded that these simple elements of fructification, or vegetable letters, when analyzed, understood, and appreciated under these mechanical principles, which are certain and real, not vague and fluctuating, distinguish the genera so certainly one from another, that nothing more is wanted, and that there is no need to appeal to the general appearance, or the habit of the plant.

At the same time Linné's examination of the system of fructification resulted in a body of normative expectation for each simple element and dimension of fructification. This normative expectation is of three degrees: (1) "most natural," that is to say, the most frequent or common structure of the fructification, (2) "differing," the structure of those parts of fructification which often differ in different plants, and (3) "singular," a structure of fructification which occurs in a very few genera. Anthers, for example, are most commonly situated on the tops of filaments; some genera, however, such a the *Paris* and *Asarum*, present a "differing" situation, and the anthers are found on the sides of the filaments.[43] A pistil in the "most natural" structure of plant fructification is placed within the anthers. Compared with this normative expectation, the genus *Arum* is a "singular" exception: the receptacle is lengthened in the form of a club, on the lower part of which are situated the pistils, the anthers on the upper part; in other words, the pistils stand on the outside and around the stamens.[44] A calyx is generally green, but *Bartsia Americana* forms a "singular" exception, for the calyx is blood red.[45] In other words Linné adumbrates a normative structure of fructification in order to sharpen the naturalist's perception of characteristic order.

Linné described this practice in constituting genera in the sixth chapter of the *Philsosophia botanica*. The naturalist first groups plants intuitively on the basis of habit. This eliminates erroneous

43. Ibid., § 101, p. 66. See also §§ 92, 93, 98, 105, pp. 59, 62, 71.
44. Ibid., § 111, p. 74.
45. Ibid., § 106, p. 71.

or incorrect genera constituted on inadequate examination.[46] From the chief or first species of the genus (*primæ speciei*), the naturalist describes each element of fructification or vegetable letter by means of the four dimensions of number, figure, proportion, and situation. He then compares other species of the genus with the description of the first or chief species, and excludes from the description all marks in which they disagree. Linné called the resulting description, or definition, the "natural character" of the genus.[47] This "natural character" is the foundation (*fundamentum*) of plant genera, and therefore the "absolute" foundation of the knowledge of plants.[48] Only the most finished botanist is fit to draw up such a complete natural character applicable to the greatest number of species, for such characters are not easily distinguished.[49] Once drawn up, however, such "natural characters" serve as a basis for all systems, establish genera entire and unchanged however many new genera are discovered subsequently, and need amendment, a simple exclusion of superfluous remarks, only upon the discovery of new species.[50]

In a study of the Linnæan genera of the *Scrophulariaceæ*, Francis W. Pennell has shown that the procedure described by Linné in the *Philosophia botanica* regulated his practice. The "natural characters" of some genera, even genera with a great many species, seem to have been drawn from a single species. The difficulties raised by the use of one species to perpetuate a conception of a genus are more apparent if one follows Pennell's paper closely. In the *Species plantarum,* published in 1753, Linné listed twenty-seven species under the genus *Veronica*. The description of the genus first published in the *Genera plantarum* in 1737, that is to say, some twenty years earlier, mentions, among other characteristic marks of the *Veronica,* a calyx, each segment of which is lanceolate and acute, a corolla-tube almost the length of the calyx, a threadlike stylus the length of the stamens, an obcordate capsule with a compressed apex, and numerous, roundish seeds.

46. Ibid., § 168, p. 117.
47. Ibid., § 193, p. 131.
48. Ibid., § 191, p. 131.
49. Ibid., §§ 193, 190, pp. 131, 130.
50. Ibid., § 189, p. 130.

By comparing the species listed in the *Species plantarum* and the generic description drafted twenty years earlier, Pennell shows that Linné drew his description from the species *Veronica officinalis.* The sepals of the *Veronica virginica,* for example, are too acuminate, the corolla-tube far too long, and the capsule too narrow to fit Linné's description. The species *Veronica anagallis-aquatica,* on the other hand, has a capsule which is neither obcordate nor thin at the apex. By means of such patient examination Pennell eliminates every species but the *Veronica officinalis* as a possible basis for Linné's generic description. Pennell concludes,

> Historically this species might well have been selected by Linné as typical of *Veronica.* The genus had been adopted from Tournefort who on page 143 of the "Institutiones" listed that species first, as seems to have been his custom with that accounted most typical. *V. mas supina et vulgatissima* traced farther to Bauhin's "Pinax Theatri Botanici" (1671), where citations to Fuchs and Gesner show its long historic right to the name *Veronica.* Still another claim of *V. officinalis* is the specific name, denoting its early use in medicine. On historic and economic grounds we may approve of Linné's choice; the genotype for *Veronica* is *V. officinalis* L.[51]

Again, the genus *Digitalis* included four species listed in *Species plantarum.* In the older generic description one discovers the following characteristic marks: the segments of the calyx roundish, acute; large, patent, ventricose corolla-tube; limb small, the upper segment being more patent and emarginated, the lowest larger; anthers acuminate; the capsule the length of the calyx and with two valves which break two ways. Pennell notes first that all species have rounded anther cells, and to this extent Linné's natural character is erroneous. The species *Digitalis purpurea* otherwise fits the natural character exactly. The other three species all differ variously from the generic description, and all agree in a septicidal capsule. Pennell concludes that *Digitalis purpurea* must be accounted typical, especially since Linné has described its unique capsular dehiscence.

51. "Genotypes of the Scrophulariaceæ in the first edition of Linné's 'Species Plantarum,' " *Proceedings of the Academy of Natural Sciences of Philadelphia* 82 (1931): 13.

Digitalis was adopted from Tournefort (Instit. 165), 1700, who had listed *D. purpurea, folio aspero* of Bauhin's "Pinax" (p. 243), 1671, where it again stood first; this was certainly also the species illustrated by Tournefort on "Tab. 73." Linné cited both Tournefort's illustration in the "Genera plantarum" and Bauhin's polynomial in the "Species plantarum," where this species was christened *D. purpurea.* Of the four species of *Digitalis* it was the only one occurring in Sweden, and hence readily available to Linné in a living state. Both from Linné's generic description and on historical grounds the genotype of *Digitalis* is *D. purpurea L.*[52]

It seems certain, then, that Linné considered genera as associations of species grouped about a type, and that he used a first or chief species (*primæ speciei*) as a basis for his description of each genus.

Linné's selection of this first or chief species was neither random nor was it governed by plants available to him in Sweden. Rather, he seems often to have chosen these species out of deference to naturalists from whom he derived his own genera. The genera which Linné has taken over from Tournefort, for example, usually have Tournefort's first listed example as an illustrative species; this holds for the *Veronica* and *Digitalis* mentioned above, as well as *Verbascum, Euphrasia, Melampyrum,* and *Scrophularia.* Pennell gives another example of this deference to naturalists from whom Linné derives his genera: Linné never saw Plumier's specimen of the West Indian species of the genus *Gerardia*; nevertheless, Linné bases his natural character upon that plant, *Gerardia tuberosa,* and not upon species which he himself studied in Clifford's, Gronovius', and his own herbaria.[53]

Linné's use of a single, illustrative species as a basis for the natural characters of genera suits his assumption that natural affinities can be represented as clear-cut groups containing relations among the members of nearly the same degree. Very slight and very great variations in the fructification of actual plants involve Linné in arbitrary divisions or qualifications and concessions. In genera among which floral contrasts are imperceptible, Linné's distribution of species often seems unjustified. Lamarck argues that

52. Ibid., p. 23.
53. Ibid., pp. 10–11.

the *Compositæ, Cnicus, Carduus,* and *Serratula,* are inadequately distinguished.

> It is often difficult to grasp the difference which separates
> the *serratula arvensis* from the *carduus,* since the elongated
> calyx of the *carduus pycnocephalus,* of the *carduus crispus,* etc.
> does not relegate them to the *serratula.* Above all, one does
> not know why the *carduus serratuloides* is not a *serratula,*
> as well as many others whose slightly elongated calyx is
> hardly spiney. One might well take the *carduus Syriacus,* the
> *C. stellatus,* the *C. eriophorus,* and many others for *cnicus,* while
> the *cnicus erysithales* departs from the character of its
> genus . . . .[54]

In effect, Linné's distribution, decided upon the basis of the simple
elements of fructification, remains somewhat artificial. At the same
time there are genera which contain widely divergent members
tied by extraordinary relations. Where Linné has not considered
some of the divergent species in drafting his natural character,
the congeners differ more or less from Linné's characterization.[55]
Both minute variations among different genera and large variations
within genera illustrate the problem involved in Linné's use of
a chief or first species to perpetuate a conception of a genus. The
method presupposes a kind of relation not always discovered in
the actual and various affinities which hold among plants.

The form of Linné's generic natural characters deserves attention as well, for it illustrates his genius for organization, and reflects
accurately the interaction of the various levels of his system. The
chief aim of the natural character was, in Linné's opinion, to establish a permanent definition of the genus. Linné's predecessors
had accomplished this aim variously, and, in Linné's opinion, with
incomplete success.[56] Consider, for example, the generic description
of Tournefort. In the *Elemens de Botanique* Tournefort discusses the
desiderata of generic definition.

---

54. *Flore Française* (1815), vol. I, p. 12.
55. This explains many of the discrepancies between genera first characterized
    in the *Genera plantarum* (1737) and species subsumed under those charac-
    ters in the *Species plantarum* (1753). Linné did not take time to alter
    the published natural character to sort with his broadened conception.
56. Linné's remarks on the "pompous style" are numerous and murderous. One
    of the best is found in a letter to the Vetenskapsakademi in *Bref och
    skrifvelser,* afd. 1, del 2, p. 272.

On this subject one has undertaken to describe, and to
engrave the parts which make up precisely the character
of each genus; and one has affected, so to speak, to mention
no other part, however considerable it might be. It is only
a question of the essential character which distinguishes one
genus of plant from any other genus, and nothing is of
so great an importance in Botany as to disengage entirely
this character from that which could disguise or obscure
it.[57]

Tournefort was limited seriously, however, by the incompleteness
of his analysis of fructification and a concomitant poverty of terminology. In discussing Tournefort's generic descriptions, R. Dughi
cites the descriptions of *Mandragora* and *Belladona* as examples
of Tournefort's limitations.

The Mandragora is a genus of plant, the flower A of which
is a bell usually cut in five parts. The same flower B is
sustained by a calice C cone-shaped. From the bottom of
this calice there rises the pistil D; and when the flower
has passed, this pistil becomes a fruit E, soft and meaty,
in which F one finds some seeds G, which are very often
in the shape of a small kidney. [Tournefort here lists the
subordinate species.] These species have no branches, their
flowers are sustained by very short tails. But these particularities do not seem necessary to the establishment of this
genus, any more than the size of the roots and their pre-
tended figure of man and woman, which Ray places in the
character of the Mandragora. These marks may serve to
distinguish the species of this genus during those periods
when they are without flower or fruit; as well as their leaves,
which are ordinarily of a greenish-brown, and rather more
large toward the middle than the ends. But there would
not be the least difficulty in saying *Mandragora caulescens
foliis laciniatis, radice fibrosâ* if there were a species which
had all these marks; thus, one ought not to pay it any
attention in the establishment of the genus. . . .
The Belladona is a genus of plant whose flower A is a bell
usually cut in five parts. The calice C is a dentilated ampule
in the bottom of which is found the pistil D; this pistil
is fitted with a cavity B, which is at the base of the flower.

57. Avertissement, unpaginated, first page.

When this flower has passed the pistil becomes a fruit E, nearly round, full of sap, divided in two cells GH by the barrier F, to which is attached a placenta IK, which furnishes the nourishment for several seeds L. The figure FIKM represents the barrier F entirely with the two parts of the placenta IK, each filling one of the cells. I know of but one species of this genus.[58]

Dughi points out that the absence of data on inflorescence, on the composition of the stamens and their relations to the corolla, on the anthers, on the structure of the pistil and placentation, on the symmetry of the pistil, and on the constitution of the seed and plant embryo, precludes rigorous characterization. The inadequacies of Tournefort's characters must, therefore, be supplemented by floral plates to which the capital letters in the description refer.[59]

Linné, who adopted these two genera from Tournefort, combined them under the name *Atropa* in the *Genera plantarum*.

ATROPA.	*Belladona* Tournf. 13. *Mandragora* Tournf. 12.
CAL.	*Perianth* monophyllous, quinquepartite, gibbous; *segments* acute, persisting.
COR.	Monopetalous, campanulated. *Tube*, very short. *Limb* ventricose, oval, longer than the calyx; mouth small, quinquefid, patulent: *Segments* very nearly equal.
STAM.	*Filaments* five, subulated, arise from base of corolla, as long as the corolla, converging at the base, diverging at the top, shaped like a bow. *Anthers* thickish, bending at the bottom, erect toward the apices.
PIST.	*Germen* semi-oval. *Stylus,* thread-like, as long as the stamens, bent. *Stigma* headed, bent towards the bottom, then erect, transverse-oblong.
PER.	*Berry* globose, upon a large cup, bilocular. *Receptacle* meaty, convex, kidney-shaped.
SEM.	many, kidney-shaped.[60]

58. *Elemens de Botanique*, pp. 67–68.
59. Dughi, p. 172.
60. *Genera plantarum* (1764), p. 99.

This "natural character," despite its exclusion of every mark from plant habit, characterizes the genus more aptly and concisely than Tournefort's lengthy description. Linné's prior analysis of the parts and dimensions of fructification had been more thorough, and his phytographical terminology was more comprehensive than that of Tournefort. The pattern of Linné's natural character rests directly upon his analysis of an archetypal system of fructification. The character bears the name of the genus described, and each of the seven principal parts of fructification begins a new line. In this way each simple element of fructification appears more distinct, parts in question are found presently, and deficiencies are more quickly observed. Linné usually notes only those marks which run through all species, and expresses them in a terminology which represents tactile or visual qualities accurately and succinctly. At the same time the pattern of the description requires a careful part-by-part examination of the entire system of fructification, obliging the naturalist to consider and to express characteristic marks to which Tournefort could allude only by means of drawings. Such a uniform pattern of description has, as Candolle remarks, only two faults: descriptive precision is purchased at the expense of grace, and in describing every element of fructification, the naturalist includes some insignificant detail. These objections, which have no effect upon exactness, are more than balanced by the utility of uniform order.

Linné's use of "natural characters" for his genera reflects, however, his failure to discover the characters of "natural" classes and orders, and the "artificiality" of his sexual system of classification. The characters of classes and orders vary in artificial systems and in natural methods. The character of an artificial class or order, resting upon one aspect of one element of fructification, is easily reduced to a single word, or a nomenclature. The characters of "natural" classes and orders, however, rest upon the concept of symmetry and the relative importance of plant parts, and are not easily assembled. Linné himself considered it impossible to discover such natural characters for the natural method, and in his systematic work, he subordinated the natural characters of genera to the artificial sexual system of classification. For this reason Linné was obliged to include many classic and ordinal marks in his generic descriptions. If Linné had discovered the natural method, he would not have had, in his generic descriptions, to describe the parts

of fructification explicitly covered in the characters of natural classes
and orders. The characters of his genera would have become comparative, or, in Linné's own terminology, essential; that is to say,
Linné's descriptions of genera would have delimited one from
another only such genera as were arranged under the same natural
order. Linné's use of natural characters for genera is an adjunct
of his "artificial" system, and tends to correct the inconveniences
of that system.

Linné's remarks on the analysis and constitution of genera
in the *Philosophia botanica* contain no justification of his statements
that all genera are natural, the work of nature, and hence the
foundation of theoretical botany. These pronouncements are intelligible only on the basis of Linné's assumptions about the "most
essential" parts of plants. A theoretical classification at the level
of classes, orders, and genera, based upon fruit and flower, approaches the activity inseparable from the "nature" of the plant.
If fructification be admitted as the sole foundation of generic
distinctions, all plants which agree in their parts of fructification
must be put together under one genus, and all plants which differ
in those parts must be divided. So much assumed and accepted,
the naturalist's efforts turn upon finding differentiae inherent in
the system of fructification sufficient to establish all genera. Linné,
in his reflections upon plant genera, concentrated upon this problem.

Linné's analysis broke fructification down into thirty-eight
vegetable letters which serve as an alphabet for the more complex
combinations from which the genera are spelled. These vegetable
letters, viewed from four aspects, afford the inherent marks which
define any genus. By this means possible discriminations are increased to four times the number of vegetable letters, that is, one
hundred and fifty-two, which being again multiplied by the number
of parts, produce over five thousand possible distinctions, sufficient,
at least, for an equal number of genera. Linné concludes that such
a number of genera never existed, and that there is no occasion
to have recourse to any other circumstance in plants in order to
constitute, ascertain, and determine genera.[61]

Linné's analysis shows that no one part or dimension of
fructification can be relied upon to characterize all genera. A part

61. *Philosophia botanica*, § 167, pp. 116–117.

or dimension constant in some genera is inconstant in others. Some parts and some dimensions show themselves, in general, more constant than others; but there is no part or dimension of fructification not liable to variation. The closer definition of a genus, then, requires the examination of member species for what is constant in the species. The more constant any part of fructification remains through the several species the more it may be relied upon with certainty as a characteristic mark of that genus. To attain these constant features, Linné described the simple elements of fructification in the chief or first species of the genus from the dimensions of number, figure, proportion, and situation; he then compared the parts of fructification in other species of the genus with this description. Linné called the resulting description the "natural character" of the genus, and he established the principle that no such "natural character" is infallible or complete until it has been applied to all species.

Since Linnæan genera began to be studied carefully it has been obvious that Linné's practice was not always limited by these stated principles. Probably, upon consideration of discrepancies between the *Genera plantarum* and the *Species plantarum,* and his son's evidence, Linné, in constituting some genera, kept in mind one or more species which he had examined, and added other species to the genus subsequently on the basis of habit, apparently disregarding characteristic marks which did not sort with the stated "natural character."

The composition of these Linnæan "natural characters" reflects accurately all of Linné's assumptions, analyses, and procedures. Each character contains seven lines, each line representing one of the seven principal parts of fructification. The subordinate simple elements of fructification follow one by one, set forth in upper case, followed in turn by the characteristic marks which run through all the member species. The pattern imposed upon the definition of genera results in clarity, distinctness, and accuracy. The Linnæan natural characters suffer, however, from the inclusion of unessential and even superfluous detail, from the necessity of amendment with every discovery of new species, and from the restriction of characteristic marks to the parts and dimensions of the system of fructification.[62]

The "naturalness" of Linnæan genera rests, then, upon assumptions about the principle of activity for the performance of which plants have come into being. The "nature" of the genus has here a narrower sense than "reality": it is the formative factor in reality. The simple elements of fructification, when isolated, analyzed, and given explicit form, teach the naturalist the characters of the genera spelled out by the hand of God.

62. See Adanson, *Famille des Plantes* (1763), p. cxx; Jussieu, *Principes de la Méthode Naturelle des Végétaux* (1824), p. 19; and Lamarck, vol. I, pp. 11–13.

Chapter IV

SPECIES AND VARIETIES

The Linnæan species concept was authoritative for many years in botanical and zoological investigation.[1] Widespread acceptance of the concept seems to indicate continued belief in the version of creation found in Genesis, for Linné's statement, *species tot numeramus, quot diversæ formæ in principio sunt creatæ*,[2] aims at the reconciliation of the fundamental units of natural history with scripture. This apparently simple and straightforward theory of origin and nature, however, establishes covertly an unstable equilibrium of empirical, ideal, genetic, and religious tendencies in Linné's thought. Any understanding of Linné's species concept and the difficulties in which that concept later involved him entails some consideration of these tendencies.

1. In English, see David L. Hull, "The Effect of Essentialism on Taxonomy. Two Thousand Years of Stasis, I & II," *The British Journal for the Philosophy of Science* 16 (60–61): 314–326, 1–18; Ernst Mayr, "Agassiz, Darwin, and Evolution," *Harvard Library Bulletin* 13 (2): 165–194; idem, *Animal Species and Evolution* (1963); idem, "The Evolutionary Significance of the Systematic Categories," *Systematics of to-day* (1958), pp. 13–20; idem "Illiger and the Biological Species Concept," *Journal of the History of Biology* 1 (2): 163–178; idem, ed. "Species Concepts and Definitions," *The Species Problem, A Symposium* (1957), pp. 1–22; and idem, *Systematics and the Origin of Species* (1942).

   In Swedish, see Nils von Hofsten, "Skapelsetro och uralstringshypoteser före Darwin," *Uppsala universitets årsskrift, 1928*, program 2 (1928), pp. 31–36; idem, "Linnés naturuppfattning," *Svenska Linné-Sällskapets Årsskrift*, Årg. XLI (1959), pp. 13–35; and Elis Malmeström, "Artbegreppet och förhållande mellan tro och vetande," *Carl von Linnés religiösa åskådning* (1926), pp. 119–132.

2. *Fundamenta botanica* (1736), § 157, p. 18. The statement is repeated in *Philosophia botanica*, § 157, p. 99, and in somewhat altered form in *Genera plantarum* (1737), "Ratio operis," unpaginated, no. 5.

94

The empirical element in Linné's species concept issues from two commonsense observations. The plants to be found in nature are admittedly individuals, but some individuals resemble one another more than they resemble the individuals who surround them. In favorable circumstances the seeds of such individuals produce plants resembling the ones that created them. In short, the characters of species members are fairly constant, and species members tend to breed true. A cursory examination of plants of the same species reveals, however, slight variations from individual to individual. In general seeds reproduce plants very like the parent, but individuals are not absolutely alike; colors, sizes, figures, and so on, vary. Linné's species concept entails, then, the differentiation of essential, fixed, intrinsic marks which define species, from immaterial, variable, extrinsic marks which are somehow unreal. Hence Linné's species concept contains an ideal as well as an empirical element. Linné's belief in fixed species is not, however, based solely, or even chiefly, upon empirical and ideal elements in his thought. The belief is imposed by a strong element of naïve religious faith. Before God's fiat there were no creatures, and since that occasion none have been created. The idea of spontaneous generation is foreign to Linné's early thought. Such an idea conflicts with his belief in the biblical account of creation.[3] It conflicts as well with Linné's conviction that all living beings develop from egg or seed.[4] This principle, taken from Harvey, and held in a very literal sense, leads Linné to conclude that all presently existing individuals stem from primevally created forebears, and that in the beginning each species consisted of a single pair or an hermaphrodite.[5]

3. Von Hofsten, "Skapelsetro . . .," p. 34.

4. For Linné's views on equivocal generation see Sponsalia plantarum, *A.A.*, vol. 1, pp. 339–340. Harvey's principle, *ex ovo omnia*, appears repeatedly in various contexts with more or less detail after the first edition of *Systema naturæ* (1735), unpaginated, second page, nos. 1–4. See *Fundamenta botanica*, § 134, p. 15, and *Philosophia botanica*, § 132, pp. 86–87.

5. As von Hofsten, "Skapelsetro . . .," p. 35, points out, this view is not found in the Bible. "Neither in the Jahvist nor in the Elohist creation legends is there the least indication that the animals—or plants—were created a pair of each kind; this is only said of man." It may seem quite natural to extend a conception which holds for man to all organic creation, but such generalization is by no means common in natural history. In any case Linné did not support his views with the Christian doctrine of man's creation; on the contrary, he seems to have considered the Christian doctrine strengthened by his arguments concerning plants and animals.

These empirical, ideal, religious, and genetic elements are all present in Linné's first important systematic work, the *Systema naturæ* (1735).[6] They are most fully presented, however, in a curious essay written in 1743, *Oratio de telluris habitabilis incremento.*[7] In this essay Linné offered three proofs for his conviction that a single pair of all living beings was created in the beginning. He argued, first, that in every generation a single pair of one organism has more than two offspring, and that hermaphrodites have more than one offspring. Viewing this process in reverse, one discovers a lesser number of individuals in each preceding generation, and at last one attains a single pair. Thought cannot reach further than this. This pair (or hermaphrodite individual) must, therefore, have been created by God.[8] Linné's second argument is based upon a principle of least effort. The Creator does not fill the earth with creatures only to drown all but a single pair presently, nor does He create several individuals of each kind when He gains a like result with a single pair.[9]

Linné's third argument is, as Nils von Hofsten remarks, scholastically subtle. The Bible reveals that Adam gave names to all the animals. Now, that Adam might do this, it was necessary that all the species of animals should be in paradise, which could not be unless all species of plants had been there likewise, for animals, and more particularly insects, live upon one plant only, or upon a restricted range of plants. If the world had been formed in its present state all the species of animals must have been dispersed over the globe as they are at the present time; in such a case Adam could not have named them. These difficulties vanish, argued Linné, if one supposes that the earth was covered originally with sea, except for one island large enough to contain all plants and animals. This supposition, said Linné, appears highly reasonable if one considers that the earth has been, and is still, gaining upon the sea, and that there are many fossil shells and plants found everywhere which cannot be accounted for by the deluge. Linné concluded that paradise must have been an equatorial island crowned with a very high mountain affording a soil and climate proper to each animal and plant.[10]

6. Unpaginated, second page, nos. 3–4.

7. *A.A.*, vol. 2, pp. 430–472.

8. *A.A.*, vol. 2, §§ 8–15, pp. 437–438.

9. *A.A.*, vol. 2, §§ 22–25, p. 440.

10. *A.A.*, vol. 2, §§ 18–20, pp. 439–440.

In this revised version of Genesis Elis Malmeström has discovered a conflict between faith and knowledge.[11] The scientific tradition to which Linné belonged offered no acceptable alternatives to the doctrine of fixed species. To admit the effects of habitat upon the natural species might have threatened their fundamental constancy. Linné felt obliged, therefore, to postulate an Eden which provided a wide range of habitats. The notion of paradise as a stately mountain derives, as Linné admitted, from a passage in Tournefort's *Relation d'un Voyage du Levant* in which Tournefort describes native Armenian plants at the base of Mount Ararat, French and Italian plants at a somewhat higher elevation, Swedish plants at an even greater elevation, and alpine plants near the snowline. In his own journey to Öland Linné had observed the gradual rise of land from the sea. These ideas, when reconciled with summary biblical detail, provided Linné, after some adjustment, with an acceptable version of Genesis. Paradise becomes an island, for Linné has observed the gradual diminution of water (*watnets aftagande*); paradise becomes an equatorial mountain that the species may find a proper habitat; and paradise becomes circumscribed that Adam may perform his nomenclatorial function.

In effect, Linné's varietal concept is the complement of this early species concept. Linné's assumption that specific differences are intrinsic, clear-cut, and stable, while varietal differences are extrinsic, plastic, and impermanent, is clearly reflected in statements in the *Critica botanica*. Linné speaks of two kinds of difference, those which issue from a variation in the outer shell, and "true" differences which are the product of God; the former enjoy a brief life, the latter have persisted from the beginning of the world.

> All the species recognized by the botanists came forth from the Almighty Creator's hand, and the number of these is now and always will be exactly the same, while every day the new and different florists' species arise from the true species so-called by the botanists, and when they have arisen they finally revert to the original forms. Accordingly to the former have been assigned by nature fixed limits, beyond which they cannot go: while the latter display without end the infinite sport of nature.[12]

11. Pp. 119–132.

12. *Critica botanica*, § 310, pp. 196–197. See also §§ 271–274, pp. 150–156.

Both theoretically and practically, Linné's specific and varietal concepts reflect the earlier work of John Ray. In an attempt to secure criteria by means of which a naturalist might attain the determining pattern, or essence, active in a manifold of individuals, Ray decided, after a long and considerable investigation, that

> no surer criterion for determining species has occurred to me than the distinguishing features that perpetuate themselves in propagation from seed. Thus, no matter what variations occur in the individuals or the species, if they spring from the seed of one and the same plant, they are accidental variations and not such as distinguish a species. . . . .[13]

In commenting upon this passage Ernst Mayr has stressed the deftness with which Ray compromised between pragmatic experience and his essentialist heritage.

> The entire range of amplitude of variation which any given pair of conspecific parents can produce in their own offspring was obviously contained within the potential of the essence of a single species. The real importance of reproduction for the species concept, then, is that it permits inferences on the amount of variation compatible within the realm of a single essence.[14]

Ray's practical implementation of his theory is somewhat more conventional. He repeatedly lists the accidents of plant form from which the naturalist cannot and must not infer a specific difference; he invariably adds that new varieties of flowers and fruits may be produced ad infinitum, but that the number of species is in nature certain and determinate, God having finished his work of creation, that is, consummated the number of species, in six days.[15]

The vexed problem of the constancy of species brings into focus almost all of the varying elements in the essentialist tradition. The idea of a fixed type, as Ernst Mayr has repeatedly pointed out, can be traced directly to the influence of the Platonic conception of the εἶδος.

13. Ray, *Historia Plantarum* (1686), vol. 1, p. 1.
14. Mayr, "Illiger and the Biological Species Concept," p. 166.
15. See, for example, *Further Correspondence of John Ray* (1928), pp. 77–83.

> Typological thinking finds it easy to reconcile the observed
> variability of the individuals of a species with the dogma
> of the constancy of species because the variability does not
> affect the essence of the eidos, which is absolute and con-
> stant.[16]

The Christian version of creation only enhances the significance
of specific constancy; a naturalist, in penetrating to those characters
in natural form which are fixed and essential, lays bare the plan
of the first creation. Furthermore, the conception of the constancy
of species is useful in combating two rival doctrines: the notion
of the transmutation of the species and nominalist speculation to
the effect that only individuals exist.[17] The motives for champion-
ing the constancy of species are not wholly speculative, however.
Both Ray and Linné conceived their systems as instruments for
relating plant specimens to plant science; fixist concepts satisfy
an important practical need by establishing a set system of reference
in the midst of formal confusion. By positing the constancy of
species, and by implementing this theory with prescriptions on
accidents and notes of specific distinction, both Ray and Linné
strengthened

> the viewpoint of the local naturalist and established the basis
> for an observational and experimental study of species in
> local faunas and floras . . . .[18]

But as Professor Mayr has also pointed out, Linné was too
experienced a botanist to be blind to the evidence of evolutionary
change.[19] New considerations entered Linné's theoretical species
concept during the 1740's. The effect of new material on Linné's
species concept can be traced most clearly to the *Dissertatio botanica
de Peloria* defended in 1744.[20] In 1741 Magnus Ziöberg, a student
at Uppsala, submitted an herbarium to Professor Olof Celsius. In
this collection Celsius found a specimen which appeared to be

16. Mayr, "Species Concepts and Definitions," pp. 11–12. See also idem, "Agassiz,
    Darwin, and Evolution," pp. 171–172.
17. Mayr, "Species Concepts and Definitions," pp. 2–3.
18. Ibid., p. 3.
19. Ibid., p. 3.
20. *A.A.*, vol. 1, pp. 55–73.

a variety of the species *Linaria.* Celsius brought the specimen to Linné's attention. Linné was inclined, at first glance, to identify the specimen as *Linaria,* but the curious floral structure made him suspect Ziöberg had attached the flower to mislead his teachers. With Celsius' reassurance, Linné requested live specimens for the botanical gardens, where they were cultivated with scant success.

The floral structure of the *Peloria* diverged from the *Linaria* in several important respects. The corolla of the *Linaria* contained a nectary located at one side of calyx. In the *Peloria* there were five nectaries placed in a circle in the form of petals. The corolla of the *Linaria* was perforated at one side by the germen, which, when fallen away, left a hole. In the *Peloria* the corolla was attached at the base and became a tube before putting forth the nectaries. The corolla of the *Linaria* extended in a roundish neck compressed toward the top, almost concave toward the bottom. The neck of the *Peloria* was almost cylindrical, insignificantly ventricose, even on all sides, and nowhere compressed. The limb of the corolla in the *Linaria* resembled a dragon's head; it consisted of two lips, the upper bifid and turned up at the sides, the lower trifid and obtuse. The *Peloria* limb, on the other hand, was quinquefid, obtuse, and equal, without any intimation of irregularity. The *Linaria* contained stamens which were hidden under the upper part of the corolla, adhered to it, and were located on the same plane as the stylus. In the *Peloria* the stamens surrounded the pistil and were not affixed to the corolla. The *Linaria* had four stamens, two longer, two shorter. In the *Peloria* the stamens were equal and five in number, the anthers and filaments separated from one another. The stamens of the *Linaria* were as long as the corolla, the anthers attaining the limb of the corolla. In the *Peloria* the stamens scarcely attained half the length of the tube.[21]

These differences were sufficiently important to place the *Peloria* and the *Linaria* in different plant classes. Yet the *Peloria* obviously originated in the *Linaria*; the two plants grew together; their outer appearance was so similar the plants could not be separated before the development of the flower; both shared a peculiar smell and an unusual floral color; finally, calyx, fruit, and pollen were alike.[22] The floral diversity of the *Linaria* and the *Peloria,*

21. *A.A.*, vol. 1, § VIII, pp. 64–66.
22. *A.A.*, vol. 1, § VI, pp. 62–63.

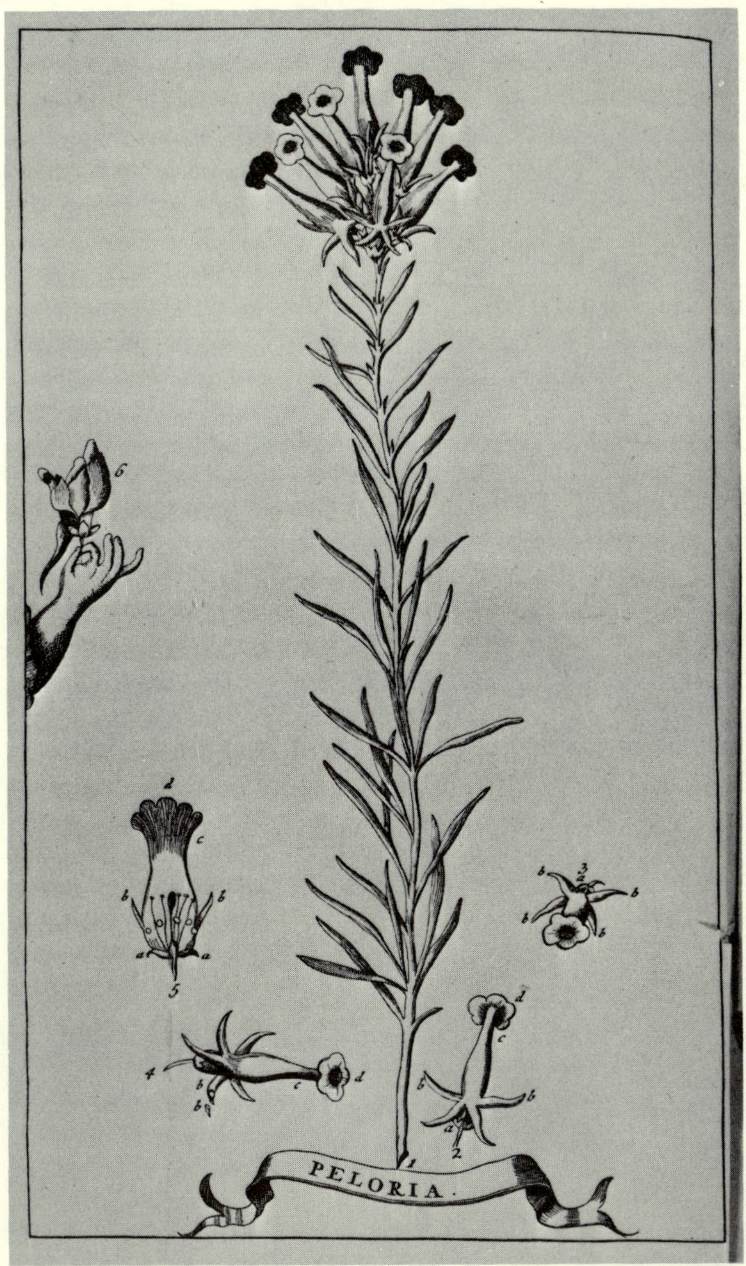

The *Peloria* from Linné's dissertation 1744. Figure 6 represents the *Linaria* flower for comparative purposes.

unlike such differences as multiple, full, and proliferous flowers, fasciated stems, and leaf and color variation, could not be traced to external circumstance.[23] Had the variations in the *Peloria* flower originated in locale, climate, or cultivation, the flower would have resembled, at least to a degree, the *Linaria*. This was by no means the case.[24] Furthermore, the *Peloria* preserved and propagated itself by means of its own seed, and did not return to the form of the *Linaria*.[25] All of this was evidence of change, not in degree, but in kind.

Linné announced that the *Peloria* was an example of the hybridization of a plant kind.[26] The crossing of kinds was not unknown in natural history. The mule was a well-known example in the animal kingdom. If, however, the hybridization of the *Peloria* could be established, Linné argued, natural history would be confronted with new and significant truths; namely, that classes differing in structure of fructification have yet the same origin and character, that one and the same class may possess differing elements of fructification, and finally, that new and different species appear in the plant world. These truths, concluded Linné, would end the use of fructification as the basis of all botanical science and demolish the natural classes of plants.[27] Such consequences seemed to Linné to call for wide-ranging and thoroughgoing investigation. He communicated his observations and enlisted the aid of fellow naturalists. At a meeting of the *Vetenskapsakademi* in Stockholm in November, 1744, "Herr Meldercreutz, who was just come from Uppsala," reported,

> that in Roslagen there had been found a flower near a growing *Linaria,* and which very much resembled [the *Linaria*], but yet kept its genus, and although this would seem incredible to botanists, and he himself [Linné] could scarce believe it, yet he has been convinced of it. He now intends to publish this discovery either abroad or in the proceedings of the *Vetenskapsakademi*.[28]

23. *A.A.*, vol. 1, § VII, pp. 63–64.
24. *A.A.*, vol. 1, § XII, pp. 68–73.
25. *A.A.*, vol. 1, § X, pp. 67–68.
26. *A.A.*, vol. 1, "Præfatio," pp. 55–56.
27. *A.A.*, vol. 1, § XII, pp. 72–73.
28. *Skrifter af Carl von Linné,* 4, p. 298.

In December the *Dissertatio botanica de Peloria* was defended at Uppsala. In March Linné sent printed copies to Bernard de Jussieu in Paris and to Haller in Göttingen. Linné asked Haller to notice his dissertation in the Nuremberg *Commercia Literaria*, and added,

> I beg of you not to suppose it [the *Peloria*] anything else than the offspring of (*Antirrhinum*) *Linaria*, which plant I well know. This new plant propagates itself by its own seed, and is therefore a new species, not existing from the beginning of the world; it is a new genus, never in being till now. It is a mule species in the vegetable kingdom, propagating itself by transmutation of one plant into another; a totally different fructification in the same plant; a two-fold character in one and the same species.[29]

Bernard de Jussieu in his reply noted cautiously "something of a *lusus naturæ* in the flowers of this *Linaria,* but nothing of so regular a shape."

> The nectary indeed was multiplied, having two, three, or four spurs; but I never met with so regular a figure in the limb of the plant as your plate represents. Besides, the alternation I saw was not in all the flowers of the same spike.[30]

Jussieu's caution proved justified. Linné's expectations of the *Peloria* were disappointed. Specimens of the *Linaria* with normal, *Peloria,* and mediate floral forms were discovered. The curiously regular pentandrous flower with five spurs was neither propagated by seed nor absolutely constant on the same root.[31] Other species of *Antirrhinum, Digitalis,* and other ringent plants showed themselves liable to the same variation. In later work Linné either omitted mention of the *Peloria* (as in the *Species plantarum*) or alluded to it only briefly (as in the second edition of *Flora svecica*).[32] In 1766 Johann Beckmann reported that the younger Linné had stated

29. J. E. Smith, *A Selection of the Correspondence of Linnæus* (1821), pp. 375–376.
30. Ibid., p. 214.
31. Tore Linnell, "Några ord om Linnés Peloria och dess locus classicus," *Svenska Linné-Sällskapets Årsskrift,* Årg. XXXV (1953), p. 63.
32. *Flora svecica* (1755), p. 218.

that the *Peloria* had so deceived his father, that he no longer wished to hear the plant mentioned.[33]

The case of the *Peloria,* however, drew Linné's attention to the phenomenon of hybridization, and from this time the mention of so-called "mule species" increased in his work. In 1751 Linné wrote Bäck,

> I find hybrid plants more common than hybrid animals and rather many in number. I believe I have been allowed to open the door to one of nature's extensive chambers, although it is not opened without creaking.[34]

In the same decade Linné found at least four cases of what he believed to be hybridization in plants. The first of these (*Veronica spuria*) was found growing in the botanical gardens at Uppsala in 1750. The plant differed essentially from all *Veronica* either cultivated in gardens or redacted in literature. In the same flower bed *Veronica maritima* and *Verbena officinalis* grew near one another. Linné concluded that the new *Veronica* was the offspring of female *Veronica* and male *Verbena*.[35] In a letter to Bäck dated September 7, Linné writes,

> The sight of my new plant Verbena-Veronica delights me daily with its observation; never have botanists seen so clear an example of new species through hybridization.[36]

Next, seed from a *Delphinium* growing at St. Petersburg was sent Linné. When the plant was grown at Uppsala, Linné believed it to be the offspring of *Delphinium elatum* and [*Aconitum*] *Napellus*.[37] Then, in 1753, Solander returned from Piteå with specimens of *Leontodon auctumnale* (β *Taraxaci*) in which Linné believed he found a cross between *Hieracium alpinum* and *Leontodon*.[38] Finally, in 1758, Linné himself pollinated a *Tragopogon pratense* from a

---

33. Otto Gertz, "Linnés blomsterrabatter å Hammarby," *Svenska Linné-Sällskapets Årsskrift*, Årg. X (1927), p. 37.
34. *Bref och skrifvelser*, afd. 1, del 4, p. 140.
35. *Skrifter af Carl von Linné*, 4, p. 131.
36. *Bref och skrifvelser*, afd. 2, del 4, p. 127.
37. *Skrifter af Carl von Linné*, 4, p. 131.
38. Ibid., p. 131.

Tragopogon porrifolius and marked the flower with a thread. From the seed grew the first artificially induced hybrid.[39] In spite of the apparently various examples of hybrids adduced, however, Linné had very little knowledge about hybrids or hybridization. In an important paper, C. E. B. Bremekamp has discussed Linné's limited knowledge.

> It is true that hybrids are mentioned at various places in his works, but these so-called hybrids were, with a single exception, always aberrant specimens that were found either in the wild, or in gardens, and for whose hybrid nature no sufficient grounds were adduced. How unfounded these assumptions sometimes were, is well illustrated by the fact that he once described a hybrid between a *Veronica* and a *Verbena*! Even the exception . . ., a cross between two Tragopogon species, is not wholly beyond doubt. The only hybrids with which he was well acquainted, were those between the horse and the donkey, and as these hybrids always show a greater resemblance to the mother than to the father, he assumed that this was a general character of the hybrids, i.e. that they were all metroclinous.[40]

Despite the paucity of his information, Linné claimed eventually that new species can arise only through hybridization. By 1746 Linné had begun to cast about for a theoretical explanation of hybrids. In an important essay of that year, the *Sponsalia plantarum*, he mentions his curious cortex-medulla hypothesis in connection with plant sexuality.[41] This hypothesis, which involves a theory of plant composition and an interpretation of the flower, is important for the development of Linné's hybrid theory, and therefore for an understanding of his later theoretical species concept.

In discussing the plant heart, Cæsalpino had noted its composition. He thought he observed at the junction of root and

39. Ibid., p. 131. In Fries' opinion the *Tragopogon hybridum* gave "incontrovertible proof for the role of pollen in the appearance and development of the plant. Well worth regarding in this connection are proffered hypotheses concerning the appearance of new plant species, diverging wholly from Linné's earlier statement: 'tot numeramus species,' etc."
40. "Linné's Views on the Hierarchy of Taxonomic Groups," *Acta Botanica Neerlandica* 2 (2): 246.
41. *A.A.*, vol. 1, § XXIX, p. 374.

shoot a certain substance differing from both the root and the shoot, softer and more fleshy than either. He believed this soft substance to be continuous throughout the stem, as the spinal cord in an animal body. And as Aristotle had pointed out that nature conceals the principle of life in the entrails of animals, Cæsalpino concluded that the principle of plant life was hidden in this inner part. He derived the seed from this soft substance, and he went on to show that plants fruit from young shoots, since the formative stuff for the seed makes its way to the surface of a young shoot more readily than through solid wood. The idea that the vital principle resides in the inner parts leads to the corollary that the external layers are of an inferior nature.[42] Linné had taken note of this theory as early as 1738, but he only found a use for it fifteen years later.[43] He supposed that plants consist of two elements, a medulla and a cortex. The medulla is the "essential" element, for it is the "bearer of life"; the cortex, on the other hand, is less essential, since it is only the "conveyer of nourishment." In his interpretation of the flower Linné derived the stamens from a cortical mantle, the pistils from the medulla. In other words, the pollen is elaborated by the cortex, while the ovules derive from the medulla.

The effective association of the phenomenon of hybridization and the cortex-medulla hypothesis took nearly ten years. In the first edition of the *Species plantarum*, the preface, significantly, mentions neither constancy nor hybridization of species; indications of Linné's perplexity must be sought in such omissions, and in random remarks. W. T. Stearn has pointed out the note under *Rosa indica*.

> The species of roses are with difficulty to be distinguished, with even greater difficulty to be defined; nature seems to me to have blended several or by way of sport to have formed several from one; hence he who sees fewer species has an easier time than he who examines many.[44]

42. *De Plantis*, pp. 2–3. See also Agnes Arber, *The Natural Philosophy of Plant Form* (1950), pp. 30–31.
43. *Classes plantarum*, p. 3.
44. *Species plantarum*, vol. 1, p. 492. Stearn's note will be found on page 158 of his introduction.

C. A. M. Lindman has cited examples listed under other genera which support the view that some species are the daughters of time.[45] The essay *Metamorphoses plantarum* defended in 1755 contains a summary of the evidence of hybridization, and indicates the tendency of Linné's thought. After drawing an analogy between plant and animal hybrids, Linné asked whether plant hybrids, like the mule, must prove infertile. He was inclined to believe that hybrid plants can reproduce themselves through seed, and that they form constant varieties, or a new kind of metamorphosis in plants.[46] Linné's ideas are worked out most clearly, however, in the famous prize essay, *De sexu plantarum* (1760), in which, having offered evidence in support of both the cortex-medulla hypothesis and hybridization, he concluded that new species are brought forth through hybridization. The resultant plant, resembling the father outwardly, is, with regard to the inner, medullar substance and fructification, the image of the mother. It follows, said Linné, that the many species belonging to one genus were in the beginning a single species, and that other species appear through hybridization.

A consideration of the numerous African *Gerania*, Linné continued, leads the botanist to conclude, that within the plant kingdom there are as many forms in one genus as have emerged from one species through the crossing of flowers, and that a genus is only the epitome of those plant forms which stem from a single mother and various fathers. Linné leaves undecided whether God in the beginning set limits to this process.[47] These ideas, which conflict with earlier statements on the constancy of species, are carried even further in such works as *Fundamentum fructificationis* (1762),[48] the sixth edition of *Genera plantarum*,[49] and the *Prælec-*

45. "Carl von Linné såsom botanist," *Carl von Linnés betydelse såsom naturforskare och lakare* (1907), pp. 95–97.

46. *A.A.*, vol. 4, pp. 380–381. For further evidence on the development of Linné's thought on hybrids during the 1750's see "Plantæ hybridæ," *A.A.*, vol. 3, pp. 28–62, and " 'Corollaria,' Generatio ambigena," *A.A.*, vol. 6, pp. 14–16.

47. *A.A.*, vol. 10, p. 128.

48. *A.A.*, vol. 6, pp. 300–301, "We imagine that the creator at the actual time of creation made only one single species for each natural order of plants, this species being different in habit and fructification from all the rest. That he made all these mutually fertile, whence out of their progency, fructification having been somewhat changed, Genera of natural classes

tiones.[50] Here Linné, following Aristotle, traced the origin of plant

have arisen as many in number as the different parents, and since this is not carried further, we regard this also as having been done by His Omnipotent Hand directly in the beginning. Thus all genera were primeval and consisted of a single species. That as many Genera having arisen as there were individuals in the beginning, these plants in the course of time became fertilized by others of different sorts and thus arose Species until so many were produced as now exist. . . . That these species were sometimes fertilized out of congeners, that is, other species of the same Genus, whence have arisen varieties."

49. *Genera plantarum* (1764), unpaginated, following the index, "1. In the beginning the thrice exalted Creator covered the medullary substance of the plant with the principles of which the various kinds of cortex consist, and in this way as many individuals were formed as there are now Natural Orders. 2. The vegetable prototypes of 1 were mixed with each other by the Almighty, and there are now so many Genera in the Orders as in this way new plants were formed. 3. The generic prototypes of 2 were mixed with each other by nature, and in this way in every Genus so many Species were formed as at present exist. 4. The species whose origin was explained in paragraph 3, were mixed with each other by Chance, and in this way the Varieties arose that here and there are to be met with. 5. These processes (1–4) took place because of the laws of the Creator which lead from the simple to the complex; the laws of Nature in producing hybrids; the laws of Man in observing what has taken place."

50. Pp. 16,18. In a letter to Bäck dated September 4, 1764, in which he criticizes Adanson's *Familles des Plantes*, Linné says, "One must suppose that God has made 1 before he made 2, 2 before 4; that he first made one species of each genus, that he then mixed different genera, from which he derived several species. Suppose that God has made a ranunculus; that this species has been crossed with helleboro, aquilegia, nigella, etc., per generationem hybridam leges divina concessam, and that proles in these between the plants, just as between animals, have retained medullare from the mother and corticale from the father. From this have derived so many species ranunculi foliis hellebori, alia foliis aquilegiæ, alia foliis nigellæ. All these may not be distinguished in arbitrelle genera. That this is so is proved a posteriori. This is the fundementum fructificationis, generally acknowledged from the time of Gesner, which Adanson should have known," *Bref och skrifvelser*, afd 1, del 5, p. 127. See also *Vita*, p. 166, "*Fundamentum fructificationis* everyone had talked about but no one understood. Linné's proposition was that of all plants' genera in the beginning only one single one had been created; that this later had been fertilized circumstantially by others; then the inner nature resembled the mother, the outer the father, as always happens in hybrid generation, and that there had thereby come into existence just so many species. Thereof, those who agree in fructification are of one sap and essence, identical in nature and attributes, that is to say, a natural genus."

kinds from the simple to the complex, an order which he attributed to God. He neither abandoned the notion of creation by fiat nor faith in the constancy of that creation. He transferred this constancy, however, from the species to the higher systematic categories. In the cortex-medulla hypothesis plant fructification is part of the medulla descending from the mother, and plant vegetation is part of the cortex descending from the father; plants issuing from the mixture of two different plants are similar to the mother in fructification and belong to her group, although they resemble the father in outward appearance. The medullar substance, because "essential," is more or less the same in all plants, for it is by means of this substance that they and their offspring are plants.

As Bremekamp points out, Linné regarded this traditional interpretation as strengthened by the greater resemblance of hybrids to the mother than to the father.[51] The cortical substance, however, because less essential, is more variable. To generalize from the *Fragmenta methodi naturalis*, Linné supposed about sixty-five kinds of cortex. The medulla, when covered with the cortex consisting of a mixture of different principles, constitutes a prototype of a natural order. Linné supposed that God created just one such progenitor for each natural order, which He then mixed to produce the progenitors of the genera; these genera, when mixed with one another, produced as many species as exist presently, and these species, when mixed by chance, produced and continue to produce varieties.

> We may suppose God at the beginning to have proceeded from simple to compound, from few to many! and therefore at the beginning of vegetation to have created just so many different plants, as there are natural *orders*. That He then so intermixed the plants of these orders by their marriages with each other, that as many plants were produced as there are now distinct *genera*. That Nature then intermixed these generic plants by reciprocal marriages (which did not change the structure of the flower) and multiplied them into all possible existing *species*; excluding however from the number of species, the mule plants produced from these marriages, as being barren.[52]

51. "Linné's Views," p. 246.
52. *Systema naturæ* (1766), t. II, pars 1, pp. viii–ix.

This speculation has many obscure points. There are, first of all, two stages to creation. The first stage, undertaken by God, results in the natural orders, and then, by means of crosses, in the genera. The locus of these interordinal crosses is unstated. Arvid Hjalmar Uggla places it in paradise before the dispersion of plants and animals over the surface of the globe.[53] C. E. B. Bremekamp believes that these crosses must have taken place immediately after God created the prototypes of the natural orders.[54] At this point the interference of the Almighty ceases.

Linné relegated crosses between genera of a single natural order to nature. The sense which Linné attributed to nature is very obscure. Bremekamp defines it "as a kind of demiurge who executes God's intentions."[55] Linné was apparently unaware of the rarity of intergeneric hybrids. Overlooking these difficulties, if one can regard these intergeneric crosses as a continuing process, one may then explain why not all genera exhibit the total number of possible species. Finally, Linné relegates all interspecific crosses to the operation of chance, and he seems to have regarded such crosses as fundamentally different from those carried out according to an immutable plan. In a letter to Bäck shortly after Linné's death, the younger Linné sums up what he believes were his father's final reflections on the process of creation.

> He certainly believed that the species of animals and plants, as well as the genera, were of time, but that the natural orders were the deeds of the Creator. . . . If Our Lord first created orders among animals and plants, and that gradually, He, in His Omnipotence, and without destroying His laws, could certainly have allowed them to mix among themselves, and from these genera appeared; and leave them thereafter to the laws He had given nature and implanted in every growing thing eventually to mix and produce species; how long this can continue it is not for us to seek to know; it was bold enough to reason about that which has already taken place.[56]

53. Cited by von Hofsten, "Linnés naturuppfattning," p. 19.
54. "Linné's Views," p. 250.
55. Ibid., p. 250.
56. Arvid Hjalmar Uggla, "Linné den yngres brev till Abraham Bäck, 1778," p. 160.

Linné, however, pushed his speculation even further. In the preface to the *Prælectiones* Giseke quotes him as saying that the Creator brought forth the three chief divisions of plants, the Acotyledons, Monocotyledons, and Dicotyledons, from separate parts of chaos.[57] Nils von Hofsten interprets this to mean that a vegetable principle was first created, then differentiated in three main natural classes.[58] In other words, Linné extended the hypothesis of hybridization even beyond the natural orders. This is confirmed by a manuscript owned by the Linnæan Society in London, in which, in a final revision of the story of creation, Linné adds in the margin,

> First earth little, for only one plant of each species . . . God created classes, from their mixture orders, from the orders genera, from the genera species.[59]

The faults of Linné's speculation from a scientific point of view are obvious, and have been pointed out many times. Linné's use of the Creator places his theories outside the possibility of verification. His speculation applied only to plants. The cortex-medulla hypothesis, originated to solve problems of plant sexuality, is badly reconciled with the phenomena of hybridization. Both notions rest upon inadequate information, hasty generalization, and obscure formulation. Nevertheless, this speculation enabled Linné to establish, at least to his own satisfaction, that hierarchic differences in nature are fundamental, and that creation is a dynamic and continuing process, even while he continues to trace the system of nature to an immutable plan known in outline.[60]

Whatever the possible ramifications of this speculation, it had little effect upon Linné's practice as a systematist. Linné continued to assume that he had uncovered the basic units of natural order, when, from his evidence, he had drawn the typical marks

---

57. von Hofsten, "Linnés naturuppfattning," p. 22.

58. "Linnés naturuppfattning," p. 22.

59. *Skrifter af Carl von Linné*, 2, p. 119.

60. Nils von Hofsten, "Linnés naturuppfattning," p. 17, states the results of this speculation: "Thus the species in a genus, would, in a way, continue to be the original species created in the beginning. What Linné here abandoned was neither his idea of creation nor even his faith in the constancy of what was created, but rather his views on the unchanged number of species."

which stamped specimens as members of one genus, and the clear-cut distinctions, proof against disintegration or dispersion, which circumscribed their specific character. Linnæan species, as W. T. Stearn points out, were defined by "constant morphological discontinuity."[61]

The evidence from which Linné drew his specific differentiae is of three sorts: plant specimens, engravings, and descriptions by other naturalists. This evidence varied in the accuracy and extent to which it afforded characteristic notes. Linné's systematic work cannot be understood fully without some consideration of this evidence.

An herbarium, or *hortus siccus*, was, in Linné's opinion, when properly made and methodically disposed, far preferable to any description or engraving, and absolutely necessary for any botanist.[62] Linné learned how to form an herbarium as a student at Lund and began immediately to collect all the plants in the neighborhood.[63] In Uppsala in 1729 he possessed, by his own account, above six hundred indigenous plants preserved in his cabinet. In Lapland Linné collected specimens upon which he based subsequently his *Flora lapponica*. In Holland Linné received specimens from Clifford, Gronovius, and van Royen, in England from Philip Miller, and in Paris from Bernard de Jussieu. Linné's journeys to the Swedish provinces enriched his collection of native plants. From Russia Linné received plants from Baron Bjelke, Johan Georg Gmelin, and Prince Grigorii Demidov. From the south of France Linné received the collection of François Boissier de Sauvages de la Croix, which included the herbarium of Pierre Magnol. Through Magnus Lagerström, director of the Swedish East India Company, from Osbeck, Torén, Burman, and Baster Linné received oriental specimens, from Hasselquist specimens from Anatolia, Egypt, and Palestine, and from Kalm specimens from North America.

61. "An Introduction to the *Species Plantarum*," p. 159.
62. *Philosophia botanica*, § 11, p. 7. Study of the Linnæan herbarium has become a discipline in itself. For bibliographical indications, see W. T. Stearn, "An Introduction to the *Species Plantarum*," pp. 103–124; Benjamin Daydon Jackson, "Index to the Linnæan Herbarium with indications of the types of species marked by Carl von Linné," a supplement to *Proceedings of the Linnæan Society of London*, 124 (1912): 1–152; and Spencer Savage, *A catalogue of the Linnæan herbarium* (1945). This catalogue is a recompilation on a more detailed basis of Jackson's MS catalogue.
63. *Vita*, pp. 61, 94.

These accessions before and during the work on the *Species plantarum* gave Linné an extensive and fairly representative selection of specimens. After the publication of the *Species plantarum* Linné continued to add to his collection. As an old man Linné reckoned his herbarium "infallibly the largest anyone has seen," and one of the chief of his merits and inventions.[64]

Concerning the arrangement of his herbarium, Linné stated that he pasted all species to a half sheet; he then assembled all species belonging to one genus into a single sheet (*sitt hela ark*) upon which he wrote the name of the genus; these genera in turn he ranged according to their classes and orders. "So handy a partition," says Linné,

> that never more handy has been; where several examples are required in a species for the sake of varieties or some change, several half sheets are pasted in and the pages belonging to the same species are basted together with a pin in the corner of the page.[65]

Linné's standards as a collector faithfully reflected his theories. One or two specimens represented a species adequately. He regarded all specimens belonging to the same species by his criteria as duplicates, and he discarded earlier specimens when he received one more pleasing. He gave away three thousand specimens, and a year before his death the younger Linné wrote Abraham Bäck,

> My blessed Father weeded out his herbarium while he was still able to do something, and has burnt up all the duplicates, why no one knows.[66]

In the preface to the *Species plantarum* Linné states that besides his own collection he has consulted the herbaria of Burser, Hermann, Clifford, Burman, Gronovius, Royen, Sloane, Sherard, Bobart, Miller, Surian, Tournefort, Vaillant, Jussieu, Bäck, and others.[67] Among these Linné's knowledge of English and French herbaria

---

64. *Vita*, pp. 173–176.
65. *Vita*, p. 176.
66. Arvid Hjalmar Uggla, "Linné den yngres brev till Abraham Bäck. 2. 1779–1783," *Svenska Linné-Sällskapets Årsskrift*, Årg. XLI, 1958 (Uppsala, Almqvist & Wiksell, 1959), p. 81.
67. Unpaginated, second page.

was probably perfunctory. In order to account for many of the entries in the *Species plantarum*, therefore, one must consider as well evidence Linné sifted from earlier authors.

Linné's secondhand evidence included descriptions based upon herbarium specimens, and woodcuts and engravings.[68] With the exceptions of the specimens in Burser's herbarium at Uppsala, arranged according to Bauhin's *Pinax*, Linné must have found it difficult to check the references of earlier naturalists against materials used. As W. T. Stearn points out, Linné could adapt one of three approaches to such material: he could assimilate a reference to material with which it seemed to agree; he could retain the reference and treat it as obscure; or he could omit the reference altogether.[69] Perhaps inevitably, descriptions made according to varying theories offered Linné inaccurate or insufficient evidence and led to the aggregation of several species.

Linné's descriptions of species on the basis of this evidence manifest the same characteristic division between intrinsic and accidental determinations found earlier in the definition of genera, and an attempt to trace variation to outward circumstance. All marks which cannot be traced to the nature of the plant, and all marks determined by the plant's spatial and temporal situation are extrinsic, and have no necessary relation to the species. Size, for example, which varies according to place, soil, climate, and nourishment, cannot afford any essential differences. Marks taken from comparison with other plants cannot be essential. Place of growth cannot distinguish a species; the time of flowering is accidental with respect to a plant. Color is inconstant in the same species and cannot be of service in specific descriptions. Smell, because it admits no limits and can be defined only in relation to a perceiver, cannot serve as a mark of distinction. Taste, which varies with the taster, must be excluded from specific distinctions. Medicinal and other virtues afford only vain and erroneous distinctions. Sex can never constitute different species. Monstrous flowers, which take their origin in natural flowers, can never be taken for distinct species. Plant armature is a ridiculous distinction since plants often lose it by culture or change of place. Duration respects

68. See John Lewis Heller, "Index auctorum et librorum a Linnæo (*Species Plantarum*, 1753) citatorum," *Species plantarum*, vol. 2, pp. 3–60.
69. "An Introduction to the *Species Plantarum*," p. 159.

place of growth rather than the plant and cannot therefore be admitted among specific distinctions. Multiplications of parts take place according to the place of growth, and such variations are, therefore, no proper distinctive mark.[70]

Such determinations, Linné concluded, make plants a little different, but do not change one species into another.[71] True specific differences, on the other hand, are constant, certain, and organic,[72] and in contrast to the marks which establish membership in the theoretical categories of the Linnæan system, specific marks are derived from both the systems of fructification and vegetation.[73]

Linné described his practice in constituting species in the eighth chapter of the *Philosophia botanica*. He began by listing the considerations behind good specific descriptions. The description must distinguish the plant from its congeners, but only from those congeners. The constant, certain, and organic marks by which species are defined are afforded by root, stem, leaf, organic parts necessary to nutrition, the system of fructification, mode of flowering, and fulcra. Linné's analysis of these parts again resolves plant form into simple elements conceived as the irreducible components in any scientific constitution of species. And as in the case of the higher systematic categories, these elements are described from the aspects of number, form, situation, and proportion.

Linné admitted that these four dimensions vary, but they do not, be argued, all vary at once nor in all parts of the plant at once; they vary, but less than other dimensions, and not so much as to produce structural differences. Furthermore, only these four dimensions suggest clear ideas and never belie the naturalist's conceptions. By describing the constant elements of the systems

---

70. *Critica botanica*, §§ 259–274, 281, 283, pp. 119–156, 160–161, 162–163, and *Philosophia botanica*, §§ 259–273, pp. 204–216.

71. *Fundamenta botanica*, §§ 259–274, p. 27; *Critica botanica*, §§ 259–274, 281, 283, pp. 119–156, 160–161, 162–163; *Philosophia botanica*, §§ 259–274, 283, pp. 204–217, 225.

72. *Critica botanica*, § 256, pp. 115–116.

73. Linné at first considered drawing specific characters from fructification alone, but this proved impracticable. Lindman, p. 49, "From the beginning Linné had considered drawing the specific characters from the organs of fructification, but practical as he was, . . . he soon abandoned this plan: 'Previously I have worked to draw even specific characters in their entirety from the parts of the flower alone, but this was an unrewarding enterprise since there are certainly easier ways.'"

of fructification and vegetation from the aspects of number, form, situation, and proportion, the naturalist obtains a geometrical out-line, or description, which includes all the external distinguishing characters found in one plant. Such a description, distinguishing one plant from all other plants, includes necessarily classic, ordinal, and generic characters, as well as specific differences. The naturalist, in defining the species, must excerpt from the description marks which delimit one species from other species of the same genus, and compose a phrase name which sums up these marks.[74]

In the root, which he defined as food-absorbing and produc-ing the leafy shoot and fructification, Linné distinguished the radi-cle (*radicula*), that fibrous part in which the descending stalk terminates and by which the root draws nourishment for the plant; the descending stalk (*caudex descendens*), which strikes downward and puts out radicles and of which there are nine kinds: perpen-dicular, horizontal, simple, branched, tapering, tuberous, creeping, fibrous, and stumped; and the ascending stalk (*caudex ascendens*), which raises itself above the ground often supplying the place of a trunk and producing the main body of the plant. The naturalist, said Linné, must not use the root for specific distinctions until every other means has been tried, for, while the root often affords true specific distinctions, the naturalist is not always at liberty to take up the roots of the plant, nor can he preserve the root easily in herbaria. Nevertheless, the *Orchis*, for example, cannot be distinguished without recourse to their roots, which are variously fibrous, roundish, and testiculated.[75]

The trunk, which, according to Linné, "increases the number of leafy shoots," and leads immediately from the root to the fruc-tification, and is clothed in leaves,[76] includes seven kinds, stem and branches proper (*caulis*), straw (*culmus*), stalk (*scapus*), peduncle or flower footstalk, petiole or leaf footstalk, frond (*frons*), and frond base (*stipes*).[77] The various forms of the trunk, says Linné, often afford distinctive marks, and he points out such characteristic

---

74. More precisely, if x be the species to be defined, and a be one of its properties, we may define x by the property a, if all x possess the property a, and if, reciprocally, all which possess a are x.
75. *Philosophia botanica*, § 275, pp. 217–218.
76. Ibid., § 81, p. 39.
77. Ibid., § 82, pp. 39–42.

cross sections as the round, two-edged, and quadrangular stems of *Hypericum hirsutum, Hypericum perforatum*, and *Hypericum quadrangulum*.[78]

Leaves, which are both various and readily seen, afford many specific distinctions. Linné classified the forms of leaves as simple, differing in respect to circumference, angles, sinuses, terminations, margins, surfaces, and substances, and as compound, that is, once, twice, or more than twice compounded. Linné considered as well the disposition of leaves and subdivided this according to *locus* (*radicale, seminale, axillare*), *situs* (*stellata, opposita, imbricata*), insertion (*petiolatum, decurrens, amplexicaule*), and direction (*patens, horizontale, reclinatum*).[79]

The *fulcra*, or the props and supports of the plant, and the *hybernaculum*, or bulbs and buds, distinguish the species of some genera. The species of *Salix*, for example, which are numerous and intricate, may most readily and certainly be distinguished by the buds and foliation, while the bulbs are almost the only distinctive marks of the *Scilla*.[80]

The manner in which the flower stalk produces flower and fruit, either as to structure, place, or situation, affords specific differentiae for some genera. In the *Spiræa*, for example, which have flowers doubly clustered, corymbiferous, and umbelliferous, there is no certainty of species without knowing the mode of flowering.[81]

Finally, the system of fructification, which includes more parts in itself than the rest of the plant, affords essential, natural, and specific marks, the two former belonging to the genera, the last only belonging to species. Generic marks are unsuitable for specific differentiae since they agree in all species and cannot mark any specific change. As examples of specific differentiae derived from fructification, Linné noted the flowers of the *Gentiana*.[82] The fundamental parts of the plant, then—root, stalk, leaf, fulcra, inflorescence, and fructification—when analyzed into their simple elements and viewed from the aspects of number, shape, proportion,

78. Ibid., § 276, p. 218.
79. Ibid., § 83, pp. 42–49.
80. Ibid., § 84, pp. 50–51.
81. Ibid., § 279, p. 221.
82. Ibid., § 280, p. 222.

and situation, contain the marks imprinted on the plant by means of which that plant is effectively distinguished from other species of its genus.[83]

In his study, "Typification of Linnæan Species," W. T. Stearn has shown how the descriptive procedure described by Linné in the *Philosophia botanica* builds upon the evidence of herbaria and the descriptions of former botanists to produce the entries in the *Species plantarum*. For example, a typical entry, the *Potentilla sericea*, consists of a descriptive phrase name, a manuscript name attributed to Gmelin (with a notation of Siberian habitat), and a rather lengthy description. Using this material, Stearn shows that Linné based his account of the species upon one of the plants obtained from Gmelin.

> The type is thus the specimen . . . in the Linnæan herbarium labelled 'sericea 3' and accompanied by an inscription on the verso of that sheet 'Potentilla foliis duplicato pinnatis: pinnulis linearibus integerrimus brevibus. Gmelin' which links it with the entry in the Species plantarum.[84]

In cases where Linné had an opportunity to study the flora in the field, his descriptions coincide with the species of present day taxonomists.[85] In many instances, however, Linné was obliged to describe species on the basis of bad or insufficient herbarium material; in such cases Linné often brought together material now regarded as representing several species. Stearn illustrates Linné's aggregation of several species with an examination of the *Anthericum calyculatum*. The descriptive phrase name in the *Species plantarum* covers a species found on the island of Gotland. The synonymy which follows this phrase name includes two other species; in other words, Linné's entry in the *Species plantarum* covers material now regarded as three species.[86] In a paper on Linné's descriptive method H. K. Svenson confirms the fact that entries in the *Species plantarum*, particularly in American and Asian flora, which for

---

83. Ibid., §§ 275–282, pp. 217–224. See also §§ 82–85, pp. 39–51. For a discussion of Linnæan organography see C. E. B. Bremekamp, "Linné's significance for the development of phytography," *Taxon* 2 (3): 47–54.
84. "An Introduction to the *Species Plantarum*," p. 127.
85. Ibid., p. 160.
86. Ibid., p. 131.

Linné represented nonessential variations within a species, are now regarded as distinct species. The entries under the American oaks, for example, consist of two or more species by present standards. This circumstance, however, does not justify Svenson's hasty conclusion, that Linnæan species are in general broader than the species of today.[87] After patient examination W. T. Stearn has shown that Linné's species concept was not particularly broad, even though he assembled plants now regarded as representing several species.[88]

The form of Linné's specific definitions merits some attention, for it reflects the interaction of his hierarchy of classes, and his ability to assimilate quickly both essential detail and an intuitively perceived image of the whole. The prerequisites of successful species definition, stated in the *Species plantarum*, are accurate knowledge of many species, scrupulous investigation of parts, careful choice of differentiae, and proper use of terminology.[89] The purpose of such a definition, in Linné's opinion, was to mark off one species from other species of the same genus, that is, to divide a genus into two or more species. Without the attached generic name, therefore, and the associated "natural character," which had to be memorized, the specific definition was meaningless. Linné compares a specific definition without a generic name to a bell without a clapper and to an animal without a head.[90] Once the generic name had set forth in abstraction the common basis of fructification in which all congeners agreed, however, individual species could be defined by means of single, mutually exclusive marks. In Linné's words, the specific description, or definition, "expresses" a distinguishing character which separates one species from all other species of the same genus.

> Specific differentiae, or so-called special names of plants . . . in the shortest way . . . distinguish the plant from all of its own genus, that one did not often need to consult the authors to determine species.[91]

87. H. K. Svenson, "On the Descriptive Method of Linnæus," *Rhodora* 47 (562–563): 273–302, 363–388. The assertions are repeated in idem, "Linnæus and the Species Problem," *Taxon* 2 (3): 55–58.

88. "An Introduction to the *Species Plantarum*," pp. 159–160.

89. "Lectori æquo," unpaginated, ninth page.

90. *Critica botanica*, § 286, p. 165.

91. *Vita*, p. 167.

Such specific definitions are of two kinds, synoptic or essential. In cases where marks peculiar to a single species are not readily found, Linné isolates marks common to several species; the specific description then reproduces all appropriate branches of the dichotomous tree.[92] Such descriptions are prolix and repetitious. It is as if, says Linné, one were obliged to represent the number eight by reckoning twice one is two, twice two is four, and twice four is eight, instead of using a single word, eight, which means the same as twice four, and is preferable for its brevity and precision. In the same way a so-called "essential" definition, a phrase both unique and exactly appropriate to the species to which it is applied, is preferable to a synoptic definition. Linné goes so far as to claim that once naturalists have brought all plants under their genera with absolute certainty and have assigned essential definitions to all plants, natural history will have attained its highest point and final goal.[93]

These definitions, or descriptions, whether essential or synoptic, set the limits of the species and sum up the specific character. Because the definition contains only what is essential to differentiate the species of one genus, Linné limited the terms in the definition to twelve, and forbids the use of compound words, rhetorical figures, superlatives, negatives, parentheses, and conjunctive and disjunctive particles. Adjectives follow their substantives and are selected from the terms of art; only metaphors which are both common and obvious are admissible.[94]

Such phrases, or abridged definitions, suffer from one great inconvenience: they are, in de Candolle's words, "toujours provisoires et subordonnées au nombre des plantes connues."[95] The definition, being comparative, entails revision upon the discovery of new plants. The naturalist, says Linné, must confer a specific definition, and then increase, diminish, and alter the descriptions of other species in the genus, that all may be sufficiently distinguished for the future.[96]

92. Linné gives an example of a synoptic definition in *Critica botanica*, § 289, pp. 167–169.
93. Ibid., § 290, p. 169.
94. Ibid., §§ 295–305, pp. 175–189.
95. *Théorie élémentaire de la Botanique*, p. 251.
96. *Critica botanica*, § 294, p. 175.

Perhaps no other aspect of Linné's work shows so clearly the disjunction between speculation and practice as the later species concept and his working descriptive assumptions. In the later species concept, Linné traces the lower systematic groups to the break-up of the higher taxa. His hypothesis contains two elements: a cortex-medulla theory derived ultimately from Aristotle, and the phenomenon of plant hybridization.

Linné, at least in his final speculation, supposed that in the beginning there existed one prototype of each natural order variously constituted of medullar and cortical substance; these, when mixed by God, produced the progenitors of genera; these, when mixed by nature, produced the species; and these, when mixed by chance, produced varieties. The implications of these theories would establish hierarchical differences as fundamental, overthrow the absolute constancy of species, and merge assumptions about continuity of form with the notion of a community of origin.

But because Linné in his practice as a systematist, continued to define species by means of formal discontinuity, this speculation had little effect upon his definitions of species, for his specific descriptions, based as they were upon mutually exclusive differentiae, emphasized discrimination at the expense of continuity.

As a working systematist Linné concerns himself with the discovery of differences inherent in plant structure sufficient to establish all species. Whatever the definitive merit of these differences—distinctness, brevity, and relative stability—they instigate a sharp discontinuity among the members of a genus whatever the degree of formal homogeneity. In other words, the technique Linné uses to describe or define the species is adequate only to his early belief that the elements of order consist of the fixed, discrete, "natural" kinds created by God.

Chapter V

NOMENCLATURE

The names of plants prior to Linné's reform of nomenclature, and even in Linné's early work, consisted of two elements. The first element, of one, two, or more, words, furnished a common denomination for a group of plants; the second element, in a phrase of varying length, stated marks characteristic of only a part of the plants. The stone pink, for example, in Linné's *Öländska och Gotländska resa* and in the *Flora svecica*, is called *Dianthus caulibus unifloris, squamis, calycinis ovatis, corollis multifidis, foliis linearibus*, that is, the *Dianthus* (δῖος ἄνθος) with stalks that have one flower, the scales of the calyx ovate and obtuse, the corolla many-cleft, and the leaves linear.[1] Such "names" were unwieldy and impossible to redact. Linné proposed a system of nomenclature analogous to that used in human names. The first, or generic, name was common to all species of one genus. The second, or specific, name was proper to a single species of the genus. A binomial nomenclature of this sort, although scarcely as novel as Linné claimed, finally brought about the separation between name and definition. Before entering into the involved question of the relation of Linnæan nomenclature to definition *per genus et differentiam specificam*, however, consider first the sources and uses of generic and specific names.

In Linné's system plants which agreed in the structure of fructification were united in one genus. The "natural character" stated explicitly the marks of fructification which ran alike through the species of the genus. The name of the genus extended over

1. See pp. 290 and 343 respectively.

122

the species so defined, bearing, as Linné thought, the associated "natural character."[2]

Linné recognized that no necessary connection could be established between a name and the thing named. Nevertheless, he considered some connection desirable. Name and plant, he says, are two ideas, but these two ideas ought to be so united that they cannot be separated.[3] An important practical problem in generic nomenclature, then, was to fill the gap between plant genus and plant name without contradicting subordinate species or contravening the natural character of the genus. To this nomenclatorial problem Linné added the desiderata stability and commodity. These criteria, when confronted with botanical reality, issued in a gamut of nomenclatorial solutions ranging, as Linné admitted, from the excellent through the indifferent to the unsatisfactory.

The best generic names, said Linné, consist of a single mark so particular and so striking as to distinguish one genus from every other genus at first sight. As examples of such names Linné gave *Adenanthera* and *Triopteris*. The roundish, incumbent anthers of the *Adenanthera* (ἀδένος ἀνθηρὰ) "gland anther." Around the six, edged, erect-expanded, equal petals (the wings of the seeds) of the *Triopteris* stand three lesser wings, equal among themselves, hence *Triopteris* (τρεῖς πτερόν) "three wings."[4] Linné considered such names best because the essential character distinguished the genus from all others, contradicted none of the species, and constituted an abridged definition.

Such names were as rare as they were excellent. Moreover, genera were often constituted from several traits. A single name which summed up all such traits was an impossibility. In such cases Linné preferred names derived from the trait judged most essential, or from some general trait of appearance. Botanical terminology provided a fertile source of such names. Drawn from every part of plant structure, such names did not all indicate equally well the nature of the genus, and were, for that reason, less preferable than names which stated the essential character; from the standpoint of perspicuity, however, Linné judged them good and al-

<hr>

2. *Critica botanica*, § 251, p. 109.
3. Ibid., § 238, p. 61. See also § 240, pp. 79–80.
4. *Philosophia botanica*, § 240, p. 176.

together worthy of praise.[5] In the *Philosophia botanica* Linné lists about two hundred such names derived from the root, as in *Glycyrrhiza*, "sweet root," from the wood; *Hæmatoxylum*, "blood wood," from the leaf; *Hydrophyllum*, "water leaf," from the flower; *Galanthus*, "milkwhite flower," from the stamens; *Trichostema*, "capillary stamens," from the anther; *Dianthera*, "double anthers," from the fruit; *Ceratocarpus*, "horned fruit," from the capsule; *Tetragonotheca*, "quadrangular capsule," from the seed; *Lithospermum*, "stony seed," from the grain; *Melampyrum*, "black grain," and from the stone; and *Chrysobalanos*, "golden [stone] fruit."[6]

Such names, especially when they settled upon some very general trait, ran the danger of contradicting species. The genus *Convolvulus*, for example, furnished with a twining stem in most species, had in a few species an erect stem. Misled by the name, naturalists attempted to found a new genus made up of species composed of an erect stem, as if, exclaimed Linné, names could constitute genera.[7] Again, the name *Cyanus* alluded to the blue flower found in most species of the genus; varieties with white flowers contradicted the name. Finally, the genus *Bidens*, so called from seeds crowned with a double awn, produced three or four little teeth in most species. Such names contradicted the character of subordinate species; they led to confusion in the statement of specific differences, and had, therefore, to be avoided.[8]

Linné wished to limit the selection of names from technical terms to such as were unequivocal. He wished to avoid generic names such as *Graminifoliam* and *Tuberosam* derived from terms useful throughout the plant kingdom.

> Such terms should be excluded *either* in naming genera *or* in the terminology of science; terminology applies to the entire vegetable kingdom, generic names only to a few plants.[9]

Similarly, names such as *Muscus, Fungus, Alga, Palma,* and *Lilium,* derived from plant orders, and names such as *Planta, Arbor, Herba,*

5. *Critica botanica,* § 240, p. 80.
6. *Philosophia botanica,* § 240 pp. 176 f.
7. *Critica botanica,* § 232, p. 48.
8. Ibid., § 232, p. 48.
9. Ibid., § 250, p. 107.

and *Vegetabile,* were not to be diverted from their universal application to the limited range of a single genus.[10]

Simile was another important source of Linné's generic names. The sight of the genus *Heliocarpus,* said Linné, with the fruit bordered by a halo of rays resembles wonderfully the sun as painters represent it; hence, "sun[like] fruit."

> The habit indicates some similitude or likeness, by which
> the idea is excited in the mind, and from the idea the name
> is derived.[11]

Similarly, the flowers of the genus *Helianthus* extend rays in every direction from a circular disk and call the name irresistibly to mind; hence, "sun[like] flower." In both cases names and plants are so united that neither name nor plant can come before the naturalist without suggesting the idea of the other.[12] Moreover, the name couples the simile and the plant part concerned; the *Physalis,* on the other hand, named after the bladder, is, says Linné, a good generic name; it would, however, be still better, that is to say more meaningful, if the idea of bladder could be connected with the part to which it applies, the calyx.[13] In the *Philosophia botanica* similes are drawn from animals, as in *Tragacantha,* "goat's thorn," *Orchis,* "testicle," and *Pteris,* "winged (literally, "feather")"; from instruments, as in *Brabeium,* "scepter," *Lychnis,* "lantern," and *Cercis,* "spatula"; from the structure, as in *Gnaphalium,* "downy," and *Drosera,* "like a dew"; from the medicinal virtue, as in *Panax,* "universal medicine," *Poterium,* "a cup," and *Picris,* "bitter"; from the place of growth, as in *Origanum,* "mountain's joy," *Hydrocharis,* "delight of water," and *Potamogeton,* "near the river"; and from more recondite circumstances, as in *Cypripedum,* "Venus' slipper."[14]

Linné considered generic names derived from simile but given in the diminutive unsatisfactory. The suffixed diminutives were too much alike; their repetition lent a handle to confusion.[15] Such names already in existence, though none of the best, Linné consid-

10. Ibid., § 233, p. 49.
11. *Philosophia botanica,* § 240, p. 176.
12. *Critica botanica,* § 240, p. 80.
13. Ibid., § 240, p. 80.
14. *Philosophia botanica,* § 240, pp. 176–180.
15. *Critica botanica,* § 234, pp. 50–51.

ered tolerable; as *Pulsatilla* (*pulsare*, to beat), from the flowers being beaten and tossed by the wind; *Nigella* (*niger*, black), from the blackness of its seeds; *Gratiola* (*gratia*, favor, efficacy), from its use in medicine; *Mitreola* (*mitra*, miter), from the shape of the fruit; *Pyrola* (*pyrus*, a pear), from its pear-shaped leaves; *Phaseolus* (*phaselus*, a boat, small ship), from the husk of its seeds resembling a ship; *Gladiolus* (*gladius*, a sword), from its sword-shaped leaves; *Tussilago* (*tussis*, the cough), from its efficacy against coughs.[16]

As in the case of names drawn from technical terms, Linné restricted the fields from which similes could be drawn. Linné wished to restore generic names drawn from the terminology of zoology, mineralogy, anatomy, pathology, therapeutics, and economy to the proper science; *Elephas*, for example, he restored to the *Jumenta*, the plant genus he called *Rhinanthus*; *Granatum* he returned to mineralogy, the plant genus he called *Punica*; *Sol* was returned to astronomy, the plant genus called *Helianthus*; *Concordia* was returned to moral science, the plant genus called *Agrimonia*; *Paralysis* was returned to pathology, the plant genus called *Primula*; *Cardiaca* was returned to therapeutics, the plant genus called *Leonura*. Linné preferred a name which had no connection with a plant to a name which tended toward the confusion of scientific terminology.[17]

The sources of generic names so far considered established with varied success connections between the structure of the plant and its name. In the third source of Linné's generic names, proper names, such relations could not be established. At best, the name might find some association with the plant genus in an historical context. Linné considered such names less satisfactory than names derived from technical terms and similes, for they were less "definitive"; they were, however, preferable to contradictory or confusing names. Meaningful names were impossible to coin for many genera. Moreover, in botanical practice generic names had often to be bestowed upon the first discovered species, yet contradict species discovered subsequently. In such cases a name which established no relation with the genus was preferable to a contradictory name.

Linné considered the names of botanists a most suitable source of generic names. Such names, already known, were easily remem-

16. *Philosophia botanica*, § 234, pp. 166–167.
17. *Critica botanica*, § 230, pp. 41–45.

bered; the honor was a simple recompense for labor and a spur to younger botanists. It was even possible in some cases to establish historical relations of great charm between name and genus. Concerning *Hernandia*, an American tree, for example, Linné drew an analogy between the handsome leaves and inconspicuous flowers and the naturalist Hernandez whose munificent stipend to cover an investigation of natural history in America bore very little fruit.[18] The characterization of *Linnæa* is justly famous.

> *Linnæa* was named by the celebrated Gronovius, and is a plant of Lapland, lowly, insignificant, disregarded, flowering for but a brief space—from Linné who resembles it.[19]

From this practice it was only a step to the use of the names of explorers, as in *Catesbæa*, from Catesby, and English traveler in Carolina, *Collinsonia*, from Collinson, a London merchant, and *Claytonia*, from Clayton, an English merchant in Virginia; and from thence to the patrons of botany, as in *Bignonia*, which Tournefort named for the Abbé Bignon, a royal librarian, as in *Cliffortia*, from Clifford, a Linnæan patron, and as in *Sherardia*, after Sherard, consul at Smyrna.[20]

Mythology and ancient history provided another source of generic names, many easily attached to the plants with picturesque associations. The genus *Proserpinaca* had a suitably sombre and triste aspect, and the name *Nymphæa* was eminently suited to water lilies. De Candolle cites the name *Danais* which Commerson gave a genus in which the female organs suffocated the male as the Danaids extinguished their husbands.[21]

The only proper names which Linné considered an unsuitable source of generic names were those of saints and the holy mysteries. Such names lay outside the province of botany; nomenclature was to remain within the sphere of its activity.[22]

Between most proper names and plants no associations could be secured. The use of proper names satisfied only the most general requirements of generic nomenclature; they were distinct and they

18. *Ibid.*, § 238, p. 63.
19. *Ibid.*, § 238, p. 64.
20. *Ibid.*, § 237, pp. 57–60.
21. *Op. cit.*, p. 221.
22. *Critica botanica*, § 211, p. 3, and § 236, pp. 53–57.

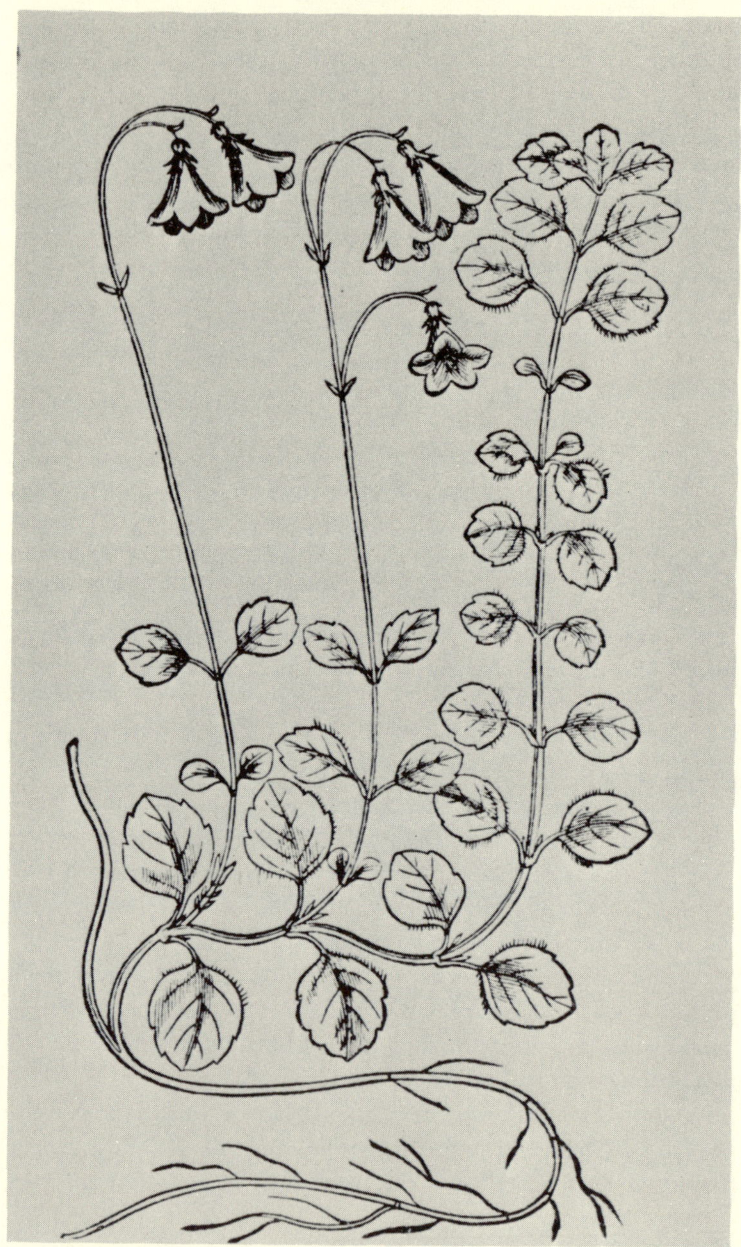

The first Swedish illustration of *Linnæa borealis*. "Linnæa was named by the celebrated Gronovius and is a plant of Lapland, lowly, insignificant, disregarded, flowering but for a brief space—from Linnæus who resembles it."

were noncontradictory. Proper names could not indicate distinctive characters or recall characteristic elements of a genus. They were, to this extent, arbitrary. Yet, because of their distinctness and noncontradiction it was possible to associate a particular description and diagnosis with them; in this respect even proper names were an imperfect mnemonic device. They were somewhat improved by three specifications: proper names were not to be of sesquipedalic length (*Gundelia*, not *Gundelsheimia*); the endings were to be uniform (*Lewisiania*, not *Lewisanus*), and pronunciation was to be commodious (*Barleria*, not *Barreliera*).[23]

The three major sources of Linné's generic names, then, were plant terminology, simile, and proper names. In the distinctions and restrictions imposed, Linné reveals a concern for distinct genera, distinct ideas, and distinct, yet expressive, names. Linné's criticism of generic names previously bestowed brings out the contradictions and confusion in which inept generic names embroiled the science.

Linné considered place names unsuitable as a source of generic names; such names implied a restrictive range which did not in fact hold. Linné was, nonetheless, a great offender in this regard; he formulated generic names such as *Molucella*, *Canarina*, and *Patagonula*, for which he was later blamed.[24] Names derived from adjectives, such as *Gloriosa, Superba,* and *Mirabilis,* Linné considered too vague.[25] Linné wished to restrict the use of the adjectival suffix *-oides*, "having the form or likeness of," because it implied inadmissible ideas. Some botanists had named a *Convolvulus* with an erect stem *Convolvuloides*; others had given this name to a *Convolvulus* with a unilocular fruit; when blamed these botanists retorted that the plant did not altogether agree in character with the genus *Convolvulus*, but came near it, and so had received a name which only just marked it off. Such imprecise thinking exasperated Linné, for it seemed to imply some intermediate stage between species and genera. Such a termination, he argued, would be proper only if all natural classes were known, for then it might mark the resemblance between things related but too different to have the same name.[26] Linné's reasoning about some compound names paral-

---

23. Ibid., § 238, p. 71.
24. *Philosophia botanica,* § 235, p. 169. See de Candolle, *Théorie élémentaire de la Botanique,* p. 221.
25. *Critica botanica,* § 235, p. 53.
26. Ibid., § 226, pp. 26–30.

lels this line of thought. Tournefort had named a genus *Lilio-Asphodelus* because the root of the plant was that of the asphodel, the flower a lily. Such names, said Linné, would be proper only if there were a metamorphosis in plants, so that from one species another could arise belonging to another genus.[27] Compound names not only instilled misleading ideas; they were a mnemonic evil. Among compound names Linné included not only names composed from two complete words, but also names with suffixes and prefixes and names derived metaphorically from one and the same root.[28]

> Can the intention be to ease the difficulty of remembering names? I maintain on my own account . . . that such names confound things which are distinct, so that it is hardly possible, if at all, for them to be retained in any memory.[29]

Finally, such compound names violated linguistic decorum. Linné eliminated two-word generic names, *Bella Donna, Canna Indica, Primula Veris,* and *Lilium Convallium*, shortening them to one word, as in *Primula* and *Canna,* or substituting other names such as *Convallaria*. The names eliminated reappeared occasionally as specific names. *Primula Veris,* which was for Tournefort a genus, was for Linné one species of the genus *Primula. Canna Indica,* which was for Rivinus a genus, was for Linné one species of the genus *Canna.* As long as the two-word generic name did not repeat itself—as in *Bursa bursa pastoris*—Linné did not object to the use of both words as a specific epithet. These were sometimes fused, *Virga aurea* becoming *Virgaurea*, sometimes unchanged, as in *Amaryllis Bella Donna, Atropa Bella Donna.* Linné considered generic names compounded of two Latin words a serious breach of linguistic decorum; Greek compounded with Latin he refused to recognize.[30] He rejected words which lacked a Greek or Latin root: Spanish *Sarsarparilla* became *Smilax,* Syrian *Ketmia* became *Hibiscus,* Brazilian *Caapeba* became *Cissampelos.* Linné salvaged some barbarous names by deriving them from Greek or Latin. Chinese

27. Ibid., § 224, pp. 22–23. The passage was written in 1737.
28. Ibid., §§ 221, 225, 227–228, pp. 18–20, 24–26, 30–37.
29. Ibid., § 227, pp. 30–31.
30. Ibid., §§ 222, 223, pp. 20–22.

Thea, "tea," he derived from θεά; he derived Arabian *Coffea*, "coffee," from κωφάω, "to become dumb"; he derived Arabian *Musa*, "plantain tree," from the name of a Roman physician.[31] Finally, Linné specified that Latin names were to be euphonious and of reasonable length.[32]

Linné's concern for stability is best seen in his attitude toward accepted and acceptable generic names. Received names which did not induce positively erroneous ideas about the nature of the genus were retained in order to avoid innovation and the concomitant obscurity and bewilderment. The *Menyanthes* on account of its woolly flower might more properly have been called *Erianthes*, "woolly flower," or *Lasianthes*, "hairy flower," but such innovations ought not, Linné thought, to be admitted; new and more proper names might be invented every day.[33] If, however, the given name were rejected, Linné tried to give the genus an appropriate synonym of venerable classic origin. The name *Opuntia* being rejected, for example, Linné awarded the genus the name *Cactus*, a name applied by the ancients to thorny plants.[34] If a genus were to be divided, Linné specified that the generic name was to be preserved for the species which had first received the name as the type of the genus, or to the genus with the most species. Remaining genera drew names from among the synonyms as long as there were any worthy to be retained.[35] When genera were combined the name retained was the most familiar, the oldest, and the one in officinal use.[36] Linné's attitude toward received names agreed throughout with Ray's principle, that there should be as little innovation or alteration as possible for names already in common use.[37]

31. *Philosophia botanica*, § 229, p. 163.
32. *Critica botanica*, §§ 248–249, pp. 102–107.
33. Ibid., § 243, pp. 90–91.
34. *Philosophia botanica*, §§ 242–243, p. 196. Linné, according to de Candolle, introduced some equivocation on this point: "ainsi le nom de μηλια, qui signifiait frêne à fleurs chez les Grecs, a été transporté à un arbuste de l'Inde; celui de βουμηλια qui désignait le frêne élevé, à un arbre d'Amérique; le nom de *Gyngidium*, qui appartenait à une ombellifère de Grèce, a été donné à un genre des îles de la mer du Sud, etc."
35. Ibid., §§ 244, 246, pp. 196, 197–198.
36. *Critica botanica*, § 244, pp. 91–97.
37. Ibid., § 241, p. 82.

Linné's practice in the selection, criticism, and bestowal of generic names turns upon four concerns: (1) a concern for clarity: the name of the genus, whatever its source, was above all not to be vague, equivocal, contradictory, or confusing: (2) a concern for stability: the name of the genus was to be proper to one genus, always the same, and if possible classical; (3) a concern for commodity: names were not to be primitive, foreign, mongrel, barbarous, lengthy, or otherwise difficult; and (4) a concern for expressivity: the name of a genus, whenever possible, was to be made significant by means of technical, metaphorical, or historical associations with the character of the genus.

Linné founded the definition of species on the definition and nomenclature of genera. A generic name bearing the associated character of the genus had the currency of a commonwealth coin; accepted at recognized value it did not need to be tested every time it passed from hand to hand. A species definition founded on such a generic name had only to distinguish the species from its congeners; the more complete character was implicit in the genus. The alternative to this systematic *emboîtement* was a long description which distinguished the species from all other plants, an unnecessarily involved and obscure procedure. Linné's specific definitions, whether synoptic or essential, abstracted and set forth definitive marks sufficient only to distinguish a plant from its congeners. These specific definitions, ranging from one to twelve words in length, and variously entitled "the phrase," "the phrase name," and the "legitimate specific name," served in Linné's early work as a nomenclature as well.

Linné's conversion of these definitions to a nomenclature proper took some ten years.[38] One can find the first step in the *Flora svecica*. There Linné numbered the species of Swedish plants from 1 to 1140, and he cited the species by number rather than by phrase name. In the index to the *Öländska och Gotländska resa* published the same year, Linné used the species number from the *Flora svecica* and added a single epithet to characterize the species. The species of *Dianthus* were indexed as follows:

38. A brief, lucid, and useful discussion of the prehistory of binomials will be found in Helen A. Choate's "The Origin and Development of the Binomial System of Nomenclature," *The Plant World* 15 (1912): 257–263.

> *Dianthus* 343 *uniflorus*
> 345 *semibarbatus*[39]

In the body of the text, however, Linné continued to use the phrase name. The practice of abbreviation was next applied in the *Gemmæ arborum* and the *Pan Suecus*. Both dissertations, which contain extensive plant listings, follow the index to the *Öländska och Gotländska resa*. In the *Pan Suecus* Linné offered a short rationale for this practice.

> If we take the Flora Suecica, Stockholm, 1745, and for each plant, in order to save paper, we put the generic name, the number of the Flora Suecica and some epithet in place of the differential diagnosis, the matter is easily put in handy form.[40]

In another place Linné repeated these statements.

> To set out everything in brief, I have arranged the herbs of the Flora Suecica according to their numbers and for shortness of study it was necessary to add the generic name and a short and less adequate epithet, which, however, the Flora makes clear.[41]

The next extensive reference to these epithets is found in the *Philosophia botanica*. Linné called them trivial names, and stressed their brevity, commodity, and stability.

> TRIVIAL NAMES, consisting of a single word, taken from any remarkable circumstance whatever, may, and ought to be used, as I have used them in Pan Suecicus. The chief reason, which cannot be gainsaid, is that the differential character is often so long that it cannot everywhere be conveniently used and is exposed to change through the discovery of new species. . . .[42]

39. P. 321.
40. *A.A.*, vol. 2, p. 228.
41. *A.A.*, vol. 2, p. 235.
42. § 257, p. 202.

Linné then compared a series of specific names and trivial names, but he declined to give any rules for their selection. Finally, in the *Species plantarum*, 1753, Linné carried out a thorough reform of specific nomenclature. He continued to list the phrase name as the legitimate specific name for each species. In the margin, however, directly opposite the generic name and the definitive phrase, he provided a trivial name or specific epithet. A typical entry lists the generic name in upper case, the phrase name in lower case, and an italicized trivial name. All of these entries are placed on one line, as in

> *bavarica*   10. GENTIANA corolla quinquefida infundibuli-
> formi foliis obtusis.

and in

> *poëticus*   1. NARCISSUS spatha uniflora, nectarii limbo
> rotato brevissimo.

In his preface Linné noted almost as if in passing that he had added trivial names in the margin so that without more ado one plant can be represented by one name.[43] The utility of these trivial names was apparent immediately; Linné's practice was adopted generally, and from the combination of the generic and the trivial name the binary nomenclature issued. With considerable complacency Linné placed this innovation among his merits and inventions.

> Trivial names were unheard of; he set such on all plants. It was the same as placing a clapper in a bell; by this means botany took on new life; now the names could be both easily remembered and easily named and written, which before took place with definitions; by this means botany got an entirely new and natural form.[44]

While it is clear from his remarks that in conferring trivial names Linné acted upon something very like the considerations which governed his selection of generic names, that is to say,

43. Unpaginated, fourth page.
44. *Vita*, p. 167.

perspicuity, stability, commodity, and expressivity, he nowhere discussed these considerations at length. Any investigation of trivial names is, therefore, more or less conjectural.

The limits of trivial names are fixed by the species concept. Trivial names, like generic names, circumscribe and sum up the species character. An adequate name, therefore, neither contradicts the character of the species, nor confuses the species with its congeners. Moreover, because Linné subordinated the species to the genus, the specific name must not contradict the character of the genus. Linné's practice with regard to trivial names was determined by these three qualifications.

When he wished to indicate that a species had once been considered a genus, as *Canna Indica*, Linné seems to have used nouns for trivial names to indicate an analogy between a species and a genus, as in *Triticum nardus*, and to preserve a popular name, as in *Triticum Spelta*. Linné apparently used adjectives when he wished to give the essential difference of the species, as in *Chrysoplenium oppositifolium*, to depict some aspect of general appearance, as in *Filago pygmæa*, or to characterize the species with some mark not necessarily unique, as in *Chrysanthemum bipinnatum*.

As with generic names, Linné apparently considered the best trivial names those which state the essential character, as in *Chrysoplenium oppositifolium*. When he constituted the species from compound or complex traits, Linné often derived the trivial name from another genus, implying thereby some analogy in general appearance; hence the genus *Carduus acanthoides* in which the trivial name refers to the genus *Acanthus*, the name *Convolvulus hermanniæ* in which the trivial name refers to the genus *Hermannia*, and the name *Inula salicina* in which the trivial name refers to the genus *Salix*. Occasionally, by means of compounds, Linné drew attention to a resemblance with some particular part in another genus, as in *Ambrosia artemisiifolia, Cynoglossum cheirifolium*, and *Campanula vincæflora*.

Where the species offers no one distinctive aspect of number, situation, shape, or proportion to be stated in a single word, Linné apparently took his specific names from some nonessential particularity such as color, size, virtue, or other sensible quality. Trivial names based upon color refer in flowering plants to the color of the flower, as *Gentiana purpurea*; when applied to the *Cryptogamia* color names refer to the entire plant, as *Fucus rubens*; and when applied to trees color names refer to the branches, as in *Cornus sanguinea*. By means of compounds Linné drew attention to the special color of plant parts, as in *Astragalus albicaulis*, or designated disparity, as in *Convolvulus tricolor*. Trivial names based on size refer to the overall size, as in *Gentiana nana*, or, by means of compounds, to a particular organ, as in *Gnaphalium grandiflorum*. Trivial names based upon plant virtues include *Nerium antidysentericum, Vitis vinifera,* and *Lithospermum tinctorum*. Trivial names based on sense qualities other than visual include smell, as in *Jasminum odoratissimum,* taste, as in *Holcus sacchartus,* and touch, as in *Ornithopus durus*.

Linné also took some trivial names from situation, both general, as in *Gentiana campestris, Lotus maritima, Mnium palustre,* and geographical, as in *Nigella hispanica, Lichen upsaliensis,* and *Hesperis africana*.

Finally, Linné took some trivial names from the names of botanists who have contributed to the knowledge of the species, as in *Tulipa gesneriana, Tragopogon dalechampi,* and *Hypericum kalmianum*.

The sources of Linné's trivial names, then, are other genera, aspects of plant form, number, situation, and proportion, and nonessential qualities, as well as situation, and, more rarely, proper names. Linné seems to have been concerned throughout for distinct ideas and distinct yet expressive names. In the preface to the *Species plantarum*, for example, Linné warns botanists not to porpose trivial names without adequate specific differentiae.[45] A desire for distinct, noncontradictory names apparently underlies Linné's selective practice. Finally, the limitations and restrictions implicit in Linné's trivial names seem calculated to insure perspicuity. For example, in almost all cases the trivial name is a single word; in genera containing many species, the trivial names differ widely both in sound and sense. In naming ornamental genera such as the *Erica* and the *Aster*, Linné avoided generalized and meaningless epithets such as *spectabilis, pulcher,* and *amoenus*. In short, Linné's practice in the bestowal of trivial names, as in the case of generic names, turns upon his concern for perspicuity, commodity, stability, and expressivity.

45. Unpaginated, fourth page.

All of these concerns have been read as an attempt to render nomenclature definitive. Commodious and perspicuous names are more easily pronounced, written, and remembered than lengthy descriptions. If names, once bestowed, can be stabilized they come to have the effect of descriptions, since they are indissolubly associated with a particular genus and species. This seems to be the sense of Linné's assertion that names have the effect of a complete definition since they are associated with that which is defined.[46] Such names, however, cannot yet take the place of a definition. They may recall the idea of the plant if the plant be familiar; they cannot, however, give the idea of an unfamiliar plant. Only if names can be made to indicate a distinctive aspect of the genus or the species in such a way as to distinguish it from other species or genera does the name serve as a partial definition. If, in addition, the names state explicitly the essential elements which constitute the character of the genus and the species, then the name becomes, in fact, an abbreviated definition.

There is little evidence, however, that Linné ever confused his binary nomenclature with logical definition *per genus et differentiam specificam.* He acknowledged that name and plant were two different ideas, and that not one name in fifty contained any essential character of the genus or attribute common to the species comprised in the genus. Linné admitted the identity of nomenclature and definition only as the ne plus ultra of botany; in practice he contented himself with more or less intimate associations between name and definition. Nevertheless, the innovation with which Linné achieved a final distinction between name and definition, the use of trivial names, was often interpreted by critics as an attempt to render nomenclature completely definitive. One of the most elaborate of these assertions is found in Daubenton's article, "Botanique," written for the *Encyclopédie.* During the earlier part of his collaboration with Buffon, Daubenton's scientific work was directed upon the relations of natural objects with man. The implications of this study made Daubenton a dangerous and virulent critic of the pedantry of systems and methods. He assumed that only what is exactly described can be clearly known, and he wished to show that knowledge is independent of names. Dau-

46. *Critica botanica,* § 251, p. 109.

benton begins his discussion of nomenclature by conceding that a name, once established, serves to recall the idea of a plant. He qualifies this concession with the observation that only when a plant has been observed, examined, and described can the name recall the plant. Nomenclature, in short, is a mnemonic art. Nomenclators, in their attempts to overreach this art, complicate and combine words; in their analyses they settle upon parts which offer a complex yet varying structure; both verbally and experimentally they attempt to reduce nomenclature to a system. But at every moment nature refutes such systems. Whatever the art, the partitions, and the combinations, Daubenton concludes, description cannot be reduced to a nomenclature, and names are not equivalent to descriptions.[47]

Linné agreed that nothing is defined unless well described, and he advised that names be awarded only after distinct ideas have been formed. Linné questioned, however, the ability of individual and detailed descriptions to engender distinct ideas, and championed systematic *emboîtement.* A specific phrase subordinated to the genus, a generic description fit within its order and class, contained more in a few lines than the most elaborate and complete description of a single kind.[48] A name associated with such an abridged description became a potent mnemonic device. Linné's attempts to render his nomenclature even more expressive, his attempt to state characteristic marks in the name itself, his use of echoes and repetitions between name and description on the printed page—all of these must be viewed in the light of Linné's hierarchic *emboîtement.* Nomenclature, for Linné, was a mnemonic art, but an art capable of great systematic development. Little justice is done Linné's thought by concluding from the striking analogies between logical definition and the binary nomenclature (and the terminology in which that nomenclature is invested) that they are identical in function.[49]

Although generic and specific names constitute the usual nomenclature of plants, the names of classes and orders and of

47. P. 341.
48. See de Candolle, p. 247f.
49. Jean Piaget "La Pensée Biologique," *Introduction à l'Épistémologie Génétique,* vol. 3 (1950), pp. 14–15. For a more cautious statement of the relations of logic and description see Ernst Cassirer, *The Problem of Knowledge* (1950), pp. 124–128.

varieties require some notice. What has been said of generic names holds true as well for the names of classes and orders. In Linné's artificial system, in which a single character regulates the classification, the concept supplies the name, the name the concept, as in *Pentandria Monogynia* and *Polygamia Monoecia.* The names state the essential character of the group and become, as in the case of the best generic names, abridged definitions. The reduction of nomenclature to systematic definition is, however, possible only when a single character regulates classification. The problem posed by natural groups illustrates perfectly this particular distinction between artificial and natural methods. In natural groups it is difficult to isolate essential characters and hence to find essential names.

In practice Linné chooses some general trait from the habit for the names of such natural groups. The *Spathaceæ,* for example, are plants whose flowers are contained within a sheath; the *Inundatæ* are plants which grow in water; the *Contortæ* plants with a monopetalous corolla twisted or bent towards one side; the *Umbellifera* plants with flowers arranged upon an umbel; the *Luridæ* plants of an ominous appearance, hurtful or noxious; the *Verticillatæ* plants with flowers growing in whorls, and so one. There are technical objections to such names. It is impossible to find an unexceptionable denomination. There are *Umbellifera* whose flowers are not disposed in umbels, and flowers disposed in umbels which are not *Umbellifera.* Names taken from plant habit cannot furnish any idea of the essential character of the group, since these characters, in Linné's theory, can only be established upon common characters of fructification. To define natural groups by mode of fruiting and to go elsewhere for the name burdens the memory with two ideas between which no relation exists. But because Linné cannot find definitive characters in the fructification on which to base natural groups, he compromises in naming these groups, and admits in the *Critica botanica,* that names must be tolerated which do not preserve any connection with the method.[50] Linné's difficulty with respect to classes and orders, then, is that the more natural the group the less satisfactory the nomenclature.

What has been said of specific characters holds true also for the names—or distinctions—of varieties. The varieties are

50. § 254. p. 112.

founded upon specific differences and nomenclature. The limits of the names of varieties are fixed by the theoretical concept: the names define and express in words some unique characteristic of the variety. Moreover, because varieties are subordinate to the species, the character expressed in the varietal name must not contradict the character of the species. In the *Species plantarum*, where the variety achieves taxonomic respectability, Linné has evolved two methods for dealing with problems of nomenclature. Most often Linné adds the varieties to the species and marks them with a Greek letter. When sufficiently distinct, Linné awards the varieties epithets. *Beta vulgaris*, for example, is followed by seven varieties, only two of which receive epithets, *β rubra*, and *η cicla*. According to T. A. Sprague, Linné usually treated the wild, the best known, or the commonest form as the species, and the cultivated, the lesser known, or the rarer forms as varieties.[51] Occasionally, however, Linné seems to have regarded the varieties as coordinate. *Magnolia virginiana*, for example, is subdivided in five varieties: *α glauca*, *β foetida*, *γ grisea*, *δ tripetala*, *ε acuminata*, and none are indicated as typical. This inconsistent practice causes some difficulty in typifying Linnæan specific epithets and each case must be decided upon its own merits.[52]

One unfortunate result of Linné's reform of nomenclature was a thorough break with tradition. Although Linné in choosing names was concerned with continuity and stability, he admitted, after he had carried out his reform that he "mustered out two-thirds of all names, set on new. . . . Of specific differences of plants this author cashiered all which had been made by all authors. . . ."[53] These former names had some use: they allowed naturalists to work back through the older commentators who had spoken of a particular plant, to make use of their discoveries, and to recognize with certainty the best of all possible names for a plant.[54] The collection and transcription of names given plants by the founders and commentators of natural history was called synonymy.[55] Here again Linné established a body of prescriptions to

51. T. A. Sprague, "The Plan of the Species Plantarum," *Proceedings of the Linnæan Society of London*, 165 (1955): 153–154.
52. For examples of typification see Sprague, pp. 153–154.
53. *Vita*, p. 161.
54. *Critica botanica*, §§ 318, 319, pp. 207–210.
55. Ibid., § 324, pp. 217–218.

secure the maximum of utility, brevity, and precision. In theory, a synonymy might include classic, ordinal, generic, and varietal names; in practice, Linné limited his synonymies to the species. After the selected name he listed names given the plant by former naturalists beginning with the most modern and ending with the most ancient.[56] A synonymy in regulation format then assumed the following form:

> PARTHENIUM foliis ovatis crenatis. *Hort. cliff.* 442. *Gron. virg.* 115. *Roy. lugdb.* 86.
>
> Partheniastrum helenii folio. *Dill. elth.* 302. t. 225. f. 292.
>
> Ptarmica virginiana, foliis helenii, *Moris. blæs.* 297.
>
> Ptarmica virginiana, scabiosæ austriacæ foliis dissectis. *Pluk. alm.* 308. *t.* 53. *f.* 5. et *t.* 219. f. 1.
>
> Pseudo Costus virginiana s. Anonymos corymbifera virginiana flore albo. *Raj. hist.* 363.
>
> Dracunculus latifolius s. Ptarmica virginiana folio helenii, *Moris hist.* 3. p. 41.[57]

This regular form, the use of a new line for each synonym, the inclusion of the titles and page numbers, and the historical order, as well as the elimination of all unnecessary discursiveness make Linnæan synonymy a valuable diachronic extension of his nomenclature.

The extent of Linné's synonymies varies from work to work. The *Hortus Cliffortianus* contains an extensive synonymy. The *Species plantarum*, on the other hand, gives very few synonyms for European plants, and refers instead to Bauhin's *Pinax*, and to Linné's early work, the *Flora svecica* and the *Hortus Cliffortianus*, as well as to illustrations found in Plukenet's *Phytographia*, Morison's *Plantarum Historia*, and l'Obel's *Icones Plantarum seu Stirpium*, and Dillenius' *Hortus Elthamensis*. The synonymy for exotic plants, on the other hand, is extensive, probably because these plants posed more difficulties and were less familiar.[58]

If, now, we consider the most general traits of the Linnæan nomenclature, the great advantage of that nomenclature is seen

56. Ibid., §§ 320, 322–323, pp. 210–212, 214–217.
57. *Philosophia botanica*, § 321, p. 252.
58. For a complete list of Linné's references in *Species plantarum* consult John Lewis Heller, "Index auctorum et librorum a Linnæo (*Species Plantarum*, 1753) citatorum," *Species Plantarum*, a Facsimile, vol. 2 (1959), pp. 3–60.

to consist in this, that it recognizes the differential function of names. Names, within the Linnæan system, whether classic, ordinal, generic, specific, or varietal, have each at their own level an equal value, and limit one another reciprocally. In accomplishing this basic task a name need not denote any distinctive character in the group; it is enough if the name rest upon an adequate description of the group; the names themselves can then act by means of reciprocal opposition. For this reason Linné repeatedly calls for distinct ideas and distinct names. Linné's concern for perspicuous and commodious names, a concern with lies behind his principle that each group ought to have one name proper to itself, not a primitive, foreign, mongrel, barbarous, nor equivocal word, not too long, not difficult to pronounce, and so on, is wholly bound up with the differential function of nomenclature. Here Linné's nomenclature rests squarely upon the merits of his systematic work. Because Linné's class concepts are clear, his morphological terminology meticulous, and his knowledge of plants compendious, he is better equipped to join a single name to a single conception. Only when this differential function has been understood and met can his nomenclature fulfill what is popularly taken as its proper function, that is, signaling what is common to a form and content.[59] This ostensive function is exhibited in Linné's concern for stable and expressive names. If a name, once conferred, can be stabilized, it becomes associated with a particular group.[60] If, in addition, the name states a distinct mark of the group, it negotiates, as it were, between concept and experience; in Linné's words, neither name nor plant can come before the naturalist without suggesting the idea of the other. The quality of the nomenclature which issues from these concerns ranges, as Linné admits, from the excellent to the unsatisfactory.

59. The differential function of nomenclature emerges most clearly in the fortunes of emendations proposed to the Linnæan system. Such emendations usually begin with the assumption that a name is primarily meaningful, then distinctive. See de Candolle, *Théorie élémentaire de la Botanique*, pp. 216–218.
60. This stability is of great importance to Linné for he conceives knowledge as static; names, therefore, are conferred *in perpetuum*. See the *Critica botanica*, §§ 236, 229, pp. 54, 37, where Linné speaks of knowledge in terms of an incomplete tower and a river to be explored. Nomenclature becomes, with such a conception of knowledge, a true mnemonic, "l'art de se souvenir de ce qu'on sçait à point nommée."

Conclusion

*T*his study has concentrated on the terms in which system and method presented themselves to Linné. In analyzing the confrontation of practical and theoretical tendencies in Linné's work, I have tried to show, not only the inadequacy of any interpretation which stresses the role of a single set of considerations in his work, whether theoretical or practical, but also that the intellectual motives which lie behind this confrontation involve most of the assumptions of eighteenth-century naturalists concerning the system, the elements, and the representation of natural order. It is important to keep in mind the main features of these assumptions in discussing some of the recurrent problems raised in the process of analysis.

The order of nature—so Linné, his precursors, and many of his contemporaries believed—was known in outline.

> He [the omniscient Creator] has settled an œconomy in this
> globe, that is truly admirable by means of an infinite number
> of bodies, and all necessary, which bear some resemblance
> to one another, so that they are linked together like a chain.[1]

1. *Cui bono?*, A.A., vol. 3, § 14, pp. 253–254. This complex and often contradictory conception, as Lovejoy pointed out, involves three moments: the objects in nature form a hierarchy—qualitative differences permit the resolution of natural forms in clear-cut groups; the objects in nature form a continuum—nature passes from the inanimate to the animate by degrees so fine her transitions are discerned with difficulty; and finally, the objects in nature form a plenitude—the diversity of kinds of things is so exhaustively exemplified that no genuine potentiality of being remains unfulfilled. For Linné, plenitude had only a speculative and rhetorical importance. He managed to reconcile hierarchy and continuity with conceptual constancy: "There is, as it were, a certain chain of created beings, according to which they seem all to have been formed, and one thing differs so

The task of the naturalist was to represent this economy in each of the three kingdoms of nature.

The conceptual doctrine within the scientific tradition to which Linné belonged assumed that by comparing and grouping natural forms on the basis of like or comparable parts, the naturalist isolated a determining pattern active in a manifold of individuals. This same grouping process, when used to establish more general classes, reproduced, in condensed form, the order of nature in a conceptual hierarchy. Science, in effect, was identified with classification. Natural objects, when parsed into their simple elements, afforded those common marks by which they were then classed. Botany, like its sister sciences, mineralogy and zoology, was the union of like, the separation of unlike, accomplished through distribution in a conceptual hierarchy translating the essence of things.

Many of the problems with which Linné struggled in the creation of his system can be traced to an analogy drawn implicitly between natural forms and logical forms.

When, as in traditional logic, concepts are formed on the basis of common marks, all sciences follow one conceptual pattern: the concept of a triangle is formed by isolating the common properties found in equilateral, isosceles, and scalene triangles; the concept of a tree is formed by isolating the common properties found in pines, oaks, firs, and so on. "Every series of comparable objects," says Drobisch,

> has a single supreme generic concept, of which all these objects are species of a lower or higher order. Beneath this supreme generic concept there is a hierarchy of lower generic concepts, which contain only a part of the objects in the series.[2]

In the conceptual hierarchy each subordinate concept modifies a superior concept, and becomes a particular mode in which that superior concept exists. For this reason, only the superior concept

---

little from some other, that if we fall into the right method we shall scarcely find any limits between them. This no one can so well observe, as he who is acquainted with the greatest number of species." Cui bono? § 12, p. 248.

2. Mauritz W. Drobisch, *Neue Darstellung der Logik* (1887), § 21, pp. 24–25.

and the differentiae taken together can define the subspecies at various levels.

Broadly speaking, this conceptual doctrine involves two separate, but related, considerations: the differentiation, or division, of concepts from their congeners; and the mutual implication, or *emboîtement*, of concepts in a systematic hierarchy.

As Cain has shown, the division of congeners is best illustrated, and for very good reasons, by abstract entities. In the genus triangle, for example,

> if one species is isosceles, the others will be equilateral and
> scalene, the *fundamentum divisionis* being here the proportions
> of the sides.[3]

In such a division, the *fundamentum divisionis* is ineluctable; the part-idea of proportionality is therefore in every case of precisely equivalent importance, and the three species are mutually exclusive.

The same abstract example, carried to another degree of generality, illustrates the related problem of *emboîtement*. Substituting the part-idea of number of sides for the previous part-idea of the proportion of sides, triangles can in turn be differentiated from rectangles, pentagons, hexagons, and so on, under the genus plane figure. Classification at every level, then, would proceed by considering the side under one of its "universal" dimensions.[4] Properly conducted, a classification proceeds down the conceptual pyramid from difference to difference, the final determination implying all preceding determinations.

Needless to say, both the division and *emboîtement* of concepts, understood in this way, remained, with respect to the classification of natural forms, impossible formal ideals. A logically tenable division is difficult in cases where one cannot distinguish between characters which mediate the existence of the object, characters which follow from its essence as a consequence, and characters which are merely accidental; the mutual implication of concepts

---

3. A. J. Cain, "Logic and Memory in Linnæus's System of Taxonomy," *Proceedings of the Linnæan Society of London*, 169 (1958): 146.
4. Cf. Jean Hering, "Bemerkungen über das Wesen, die Wesenheit und die Idee," *Jahrbuch für Philosophie und phänomenologische Forschung* (1921), pp. 508–521.

in a single conceptual pyramid requires an initial decisive difference which, as Adanson was to point out, does not exist in natural forms.[5] Nevertheless, these formal requirements regulated the systematic aspirations of natural history throughout the eighteenth century, and it would be impossible to overestimate their importance for the form and intention of the Linnæan system.

To arrive at the essential parts of plants as a basis for division, Linné used a speculative physiology based upon Aristotelian principles similar in almost every detail to the analysis used by Cæsalpino a century and a half earlier. Plants have a vegetative vital principle; that is, they carry out the function of nutrition, tending toward the preservation of the individual, and the function of reproduction, tending toward the preservation of the kind. All plant parts must be involved in one of these two functions, and analysis will reveal for each particular part its role in one of the two organic systems with which the vital functions are carried out.

Within each system the relative importance of each part is calculated by means of the a priori notion of finality. Reproduction, for example, is essentially constituted by fertilization; therefore the organs of fertilization are more essential than the calyx and the corolla. The female organ, in turn, is more important than the male, for after fertilization the seed and its envelope remain, and again the former is clearly more important than the latter. The same process of reasoning, when applied to the seed, shows that the plant embryo is the most important part in the function of reproduction, the end, so to speak, of the whole process. A similar analysis might be made of the nutritive function, but since the essential nutritive organs in fact manifest few sensible differences, and since the primary division into woody and herbaceous plants leads to the separation of closely related forms, Linné "quietly dropped," says Cain, "all reference to the primary division of plants into woody and non-woody,"[6] and insisted upon the essentiality of the system of fructification and its preeminence as an instrument of classification. He spoke of fruit and flower as the *fundamentum* of any method, and as the *essentia* of the plant. He wished to

<hr>

5. Michel Adanson, "Preface Istorike sur l'état ancien et actuel de la Botanike," *Famille des Plantes* (1763), p. cccxiii.
6. "Function and Taxonomic Importance," *Systematics Association Publication* No. 3 (1959): 6.

use the system of fructification as his *fundamentum divisionis* in order to arrive at the essence of the plant; the natural characters of his genera and the essential characters of his species pretend to state the essence of the definienda.

The equivocations in which Linné found himself involved on this point are, as both Cain and Bremekamp have pointed out, precisely the same as those discovered earlier in Cæsalpino's system. The parts upon which Linnæan division rests play an important or essential role in the life of the plant, but the marks derived from that part for purposes of classification do not fulfill this condition. "It seems hardly probable," says Bremekamp,

> that [Linné] would not have seen that the characters on which he based his sexual system, viz. the numbers of the stamens and carpels, their freedom or coalescence, etc., could hardly be of importance in the life of the plants. . . .[7]

Accordingly, Linné confined himself to the statement that his marks are taken from parts of functional importance. A concession of this sort does not, of course, preserve much more than the external form of essential definition, since the functional importance of a part rests upon the functional importance of some of the marks, and these alone, if essential definition were to preserve its integrity, should serve as the basis for division.[8]

Besides this imperfect theoretical rationale, Linné offered a practical justification for his choice of the reproductive system of plants as the basis of his divisions. Not only is the use of fructification justified because it approaches the essence of the plant; the system of fructification also offers sufficient and varied marks of appreciably equal value suitable to the constitution of plant groups. De Candolle stated this practical advantage even more tersely: only the reproductive system offers marks both varied and obvious.[9] On the basis of such statements, Sachs went so far as to argue that the sexual system of classification would have had the same value for purposes of classification if the stamens had nothing

---

7. C. E. B. Bremekamp, "A Re-examination of Cæsalpino's System," *Acta Botanica Neerlandica*, 1 (4): 583.
8. Ibid., p. 584.
9. *Théorie élémentaire de la Botanique*, p. 66.

to do with propagation, or if their sexual significance were quite unknown. This devastating—and in the end unanswerable—criticism points up the discrepancies between Linné's formal theory of division and the equally important exigencies of fact. There is in the plant kingdom a difference between taxonomic and functional importance; only by using marks which were themselves indifferent, but which derived from functionally important parts, could Linné cover the discrepancy of structure and function and preserve the semblance of essential definition.

Linné's exclusive use of the plant reproductive system for purposes of division had its repercussions upon the related problem of *emboîtement*. Cain notes that Linné does not relegate plants to a genus because they agree in certain characters, and then to a species of that genus because they agree in other characters which have no connection with the first.[10] Each subordinate concept modifies the immediately superior concept and becomes a specific mode in which the superior concept exists. The sexual system of classification, for example, rests upon those same parts of fructification which establish the immediately subordinate genera. And since the stamens and pistils upon which the classes and orders in the sexual system of classification rest are the "most essential" parts in the system of fructification, they provide an acceptable ground for the modifications of the genera. The formal requirements of *emboîtement* seem to explain as well, at least in part, Linné's adherence to the reproductive system in his natural method. If a natural class or an order is to make intelligible a genus by setting forth the basis of its special form, it is important that these groups rest upon one functional system. To form the natural orders and classes upon the system of vegetation, for example, and then to form the genera upon the system of fructification, would destroy the coherence and intelligibility of the system. Classes and orders must, therefore, be constituted from those same elements of the reproductive system which afford so firm a basis for the genera. As we have seen, however, Linné in this instance found the austere requirements of his formal theory unrealizable. The natural classes and orders are not defined in the Linnæan system; the limitation of admissible characters to the parts

10. "Logic and Memory in Linnæus's System of Taxonomy," p. 148.

of fructification made it impossible for Linné to discover any grouping of genera less artificial than the system based upon stamens and pistils. At a humbler level, *emboîtement* dictates the order of the binomial nomenclature. A generic name, says Linné, must precede the specific difference for the reason that the naturalist requires to know what is to be distinguished before touching the species. These various manifestations of the problem of *emboîtement* imply a strong faith in the intelligibility of organic nature. For if classification could be carried out strictly in accordance with the requirements of *emboîtement*, a naturalist could contemplate plants, indeed, all natural objects, in Adanson's terms, "come une degradation d'un même genre suivant une ligne droite," in which the final determination would imply all preceding determinations.[11]

A third example of the significance of purely formal considerations for Linné's system is the overall ordering he imposes upon concepts. In the cortex-medulla hypothesis, as well as in the *Philosophia botanica*, Linné insists that a proper arrangement must pass from simple forms to the complex, an order which in traditional logic parallels the process through which substance unfolds itself in special forms of being.[12]

These three formal considerations, division, *emboîtement*, and overall order, and their effects upon the Linnæan system show, I believe, that in the very conception of a system of nature, Linné, like many of his precursors and contemporaries, drew an analogy between logical and natural forms—an analogy which, even when its logical substance had disappeared, continued to confer upon the system an appearance of rational justification, a rebarbative formalism, as Buffon remarked, which rendered "la langue de la science plus difficile que la science même."[13]

Beyond these three important formal considerations, further confirmation of the existence of this analogy must be sought in the linguistic detail with which Linné presents his system. Piaget, for example, notes a certain resemblance between binary nomenclature and logical definition *per genus et differentiam specificam*.[14] Dau-

11. P. cccxxiv.
12. Cf. Carl Prantl, *Geschichte der Logik im Abendlande* (1855), pp. 210–263.
13. Georges Louis de Buffon, *Histoire naturelle générale* (1749–1767), p. 9.
14. Jean Piaget, "La Pensée Biologique," *Introduction à l'Épistémologie Génétique*, vol. 3 (1950), p. 15.

din has pointed out an overt parallel with class logic drawn by
Linné in justifying the set structure of his system. In the *Philosophia
botanica* Linné defines a system as a guide in botany consisting
of five members, class, order, genus, species, and variety.[15] In the
Systema naturæ Linné repeats these assertions: the science of nature
supposes a systematic arrangement of bodies, and this systematic
arrangement consists of five subordinate groups.[16] Linné's justification of this fixed series is practical: such a system allows the naturalist to follow a regular order of signs and to attain the genera
and species upon which all true natural knowledge depends. The
intercalation of a fixed number of formal units between the kingdom and the individual issues primarily, then, from a concern
for clarity and regularity.[17] Linné justifies the choice of the number
five by other means, however. He draws three analogies between
botany and other sciences which also make use of five fundamental
terms. Geography passes from kingdom to canton through the
intervening province, territory, and district; military science passes
from legion to soldier by means of cohort, maniple, and squad;
and philosophy passes from *genus summum* to *individuum* by means
of *intermedium*, *proximum*, and *species*. Of this final analogy Daudin
remarks,

> This latter series, although far removed, in itself, from the
> needs of the argument, might actually very well have been
> for him a motive for limiting the series of taxonomic units
> to five terms.[18]

This speculation cannot be pushed too far, for Linné, in drawing
the analogies, disdains explanation. In the light of the speculative
problems already examined, however, Daudin's conjecture acquires
plausibility. Where a likeness between natural and logical forms
is thought to exist, it is reasonable to assume that the limited
series of logical abstraction exhaust the order of nature as well.

15. § 155, p. 98.
16. *Systema naturæ* (1766), p. 6.
17. The alternative, a synopsis, or a number of dichotomies varying from one
    section to another, was advocated by Aristotle, who refused to institute
    uniform subordination where unequal degrees of affinity existed. See Jür-
    gen Bona Meyer, *Aristoteles Thierkunde* (1855), p. 328.
18. Henri Daudin, De Linné *à Jussieu* (1740–1790), p. 38, n. 1.

Further evidence for Linné's belief in an analogy of logical and natural forms can be found in the metaphors with which he characterizes appearance, nature, and science. He speaks of sensible nature as a cryptogram, and seeks to isolate the formative factor of the cryptogram in a key, the natural method.[19] He compares nature to a labyrinth and scientific method to the thread of Ariadne.[20] He compares plant organography to an alphabet spelled out by the hand of God to be read off by the naturalist as knowledge.[21] These metaphors, nature as hieroglyph, labyrinth, and alphabet, are found in the work of many naturalists of the Enlightenment. They are metaphors which occur spontaneously, as it were, to thinkers convinced of the fundamental rationality of nature.

Even in Linné's own century scientists expressed serious doubts whether the system of nature is well compared to the conceptual hierarchy of an Aristotelian class logic, whether natural forms offer a fundamental difference upon which to operate a class *emboîtement*, and finally, whether one can ever attain a statement of essence in situations where one cannot distinguish between essence, property, and accident. Nevertheless, that Linné should proceed as if there were a fundamental similitude between natural and logical forms, argues an incontrovertible faith in the rationality and intelligibility of nature.

It is precisely this conviction which makes Linné's scientific work something of a religious enterprise. Rational inquiry must inevitably, in Linné's opinion, lead, not to scepticism or disbelief, but to the acknowledgement of and respect for an omniscient and omnipotent Creator. This idea, implicit in all of Linné's work, is the exclusive theme of two important essays, the *Curiositas naturalis* (1748), and the *Politia naturæ* (1760).

Curiositas naturalis, which treats of the relation between natural science and religion,[22] opens with one of those curious surveys, half poetry, half pedantry, with which Linné so potently conveys his wonder at the diversity and complexity of nature. He passes from the stone dwellings of coral to the plantain tree, from fossil shells to butterflies, from lilies to hawks, in his attempt to show

19. *Classes plantarum*, p. 487, no. 13.
20. *Philosophia botanica*, § 156, p. 98.
21. "Ratio operis," *Genera plantarum* (1737), unpaginated, fifth page, no. 11.
22. *A.A.*, vol. 1, pp. 541–564.

that the objects in nature are as an endless sea, and that man's wisdom scarce suffices to investigate the foot of a fly. Man, says Linné, need not wish for new worlds and new wonders, for this world is so great that it surpasses our ability to explore its surface, and so intricate that we cannot understand the artful construction of the least of its denizens.

Had God chosen, Linné continues, He might have created everything for the sustenance of man in one formless mass; but it was God's intention to place before man's eyes a plentitude of new and admirable objects; in man God implanted the curiosity to inquire who he is, whence he comes, whither he is going, for what purpose he is created, and by whose benevolence he is preserved. This faculty of curiosity, when cultivated and systematized, becomes natural history, a science which teaches us to see the Creator glorified in His work, and to discover His intention by comparing His works. That the lessons of this science agree remarkably well with scripture need not surprise us, for both nature and revelation have one source. Wherever we turn, reason, revelation, and experience conspire to show that all things are created for a purpose; that nature was created for the sake of man; that the function of man is an activity of the soul which implies a rational principle; and that man has been given reason and speech to know his Maker and to sing His praise.

The *Politia naturæ*,[23] a theodicy, purveys that reasoned acquiescence in the inevitable, as Lovejoy describes it, which rests upon the conviction that the inevitability is absolute.[24] The economy of nature, Linné explains, consists of an infinite number of bodies, all necessary, and all linked together like a chain. Since any gap in this chain inevitably destroys the order of nature, it follows that the most apparent evil in nature is constitutional. For the three kingdoms of nature in their cyclical repetitions of propagation, conservation, and destruction, survive by preying upon one another, and all creatures, therefore, necessarily crowd upon, restrict, and come into conflict with one another. Hence the paradox: from the war of all against all which appears so great an evil there issues a good, the order and balance of nature.

But when examined from a more enlightened point of view the paradox vanishes. The state of nature may be likened to a

23. *A.A.*, vol. 6, pp. 17–39.
24. Arthur O. Lovejoy, *The Great Chain of Being* (1936), p. 221.

monarchy in which the ruler is the first servant of the state, a ruler who manifests his power in restraining the great, leaving his lesser subjects to his servants. In such a state it is a mistake to say that the lesser are created only for the benefit of the greater: all subjects have their appointed stations and tasks. Just as all subjects honor their ruler and lighten his burden by performing their proper tasks, so all things in nature contribute to the honor of man, if often indirectly, by accomplishing their peculiar functions. And man, the first servant of nature, accomplishes his proper task in surveying and praising God's creation.

These dissertations, *Curiositas naturalis* and *Politia naturæ*, are characteristic expressions of the reluctant secularity of Linné's thought. In them the independence of the sciences of natural history manifests itself in the attempt to grasp nature by approaching it as an organic whole, self-sustaining and self-explanatory. If, in many respects, Linné's conception of nature, his method, and his use of the concept of purpose still betray the desire to achieve the "explanation" of nature, nevertheless, Linné here clearly recognizes and states as fact that the physical and moral order of things can only be approached by reasoning rightly upon experience.

The awkward juxtaposition of systematic and speculative material in these concluding remarks exemplifies, in its way, something of the range and nature of Linné's work, a miscellany in which one discovers by turns the scrupulous observations of a laborious scholastic and the sweeping views of an ardent genius. The variant modes of expression, however, are only so many refractions of Linné's central conviction that reason, objectified in science and in a society shaped by science, can attain, through knowledge of the self, of the world, and of God, the only life worthy of being lived.

This conviction, like all good eighteenth-century convictions is epitomized in a moral. Linné reiterates on every occasion that the discovery of the order of nature is the task of man, the eye and reason of the world. The true aim of human existence, for Linné, is knowledge, and the true aim of knowledge is the discovery of the intelligible as it is manifest in things felt and seen. In sensible appearance and the sport of outward form, Linné seeks the inward shell and original limits of nature.

Appendix

LINNÉ'S METHOD

*I*n 1736 Linné published a broadside entitled *Caroli Linnæi, Sveci, Methodus*. This sheet, here reproduced, was inserted in copies of the first edition of the *Systema naturæ*, and reprinted in the second to ninth editions.

THE METHOD OF CARL VON LINNÉ, THE SWEDE, by which the Physiologist can accurately and successfully put together the history of each and every natural object, which method is contained in the following paragraphs.

I. Names

1. Give the selected name, both generic and specific, of the author, if already described, or give a name oneself.
2. List the synonyms of all the important systematists.
3. List as far as possible the synonyms of all the older or more recent authors.
4. Give the vernacular name, also translated into Latin.
5. List the names given by various peoples, especially the Greek names.
6. State the etymology of all generic names (1–5).

II. Theory

7. Discuss the classifications as to classes and orders according to different systems.
8. State the genera to which the object in question has been assigned by the various systematists (7).

III. Genus

9. Give an account of the natural characters, with a list of all possible characteristic features.
10. Give the essential characters, pointing out the most distinguishing features.
11. Set forth also artificial characters in order to distinguish the genera treated as units in the systems (7).
12. Explain the erroneous ideas of the authors discussed under (8) in the light of (9).
13. Establish the natural genus (9).
14. The name of the genus (13), as selected by (1), is to be confirmed, and it is to be stated why other names are rejected.

IV. Species

15. A detailed description of the object is to be given, based on all its external parts.
16. All the known species of the proposed genus (13) are to be listed.
17. All the differences between the proposed species (1), and the ones listed (16) are to be set forth (15).
18. The important differences shall then be retained, and the others rejected.
19. The specific differences with the reason for what has been done until the naturalist has fully accounted for every word in it.
20. All the variations of the proposed species, as described by the authors quoted, are to be set forth.
21. These variations are to be subordinated to the species to which they naturally belong, with the reason for the action proposed under paragraph (15).

V. Attributes

22. Include what is known about the season of birth, growth, and maturity, with mode of breeding and of birth or hatching, old age, and death.
23. State the locality, giving the geographic region and political province.

24. Give the latitude and longitude.
25. Describe the climate and the soil.
26. Give an account of the diet, habits, and temperament.
27. Describe the anatomy of the body, particularly any remarkable features, together with a microscopic examination.

VI. Uses

28. List the economic uses, actual and possible, among various peoples.
29. State dietary uses, with the effects on the human body.
30. State the physical uses, with the mode of operation and the constituent elements.
31. State the chemical uses according to the constituent substances from analysis.
32. State the medical uses, in which diseases, and with what results, according to reason and experience.
33. Give the pharmaceutical information, as to what parts are used, method of preparation, and composition.
34. Give the directions for medical use, with emphasis on the best method, dosage, and necessary precautions.

VII. Literature

35. The collector, with place and time, is to be noted.
36. Amusing and pleasing historical traditions are to be reported.
37. Empty superstitions are to be rejected.
38. Selected poetic references to be cited.[1]

---

1. This translation taken from *Species plantarum, a Facsimile of the first edition 1753* (1959), vol. 2, pp. 75–80.

Books and Memoirs Cited

I.   Works of Carl von Linné

Amoenitates academicæ seu dissertationes variæ physicæ, medicæ botanicae antehac seorsim editæ nunc collectæ et auctæ cum tabulis æneis. 10 vols. . . . curante Jo. Christiano Daniele Schrebero . . . Erlangæ sumtu Jo. Jacobi Palm, 1785–1789.

The following dissertations have been cited:

Vol. 1

Peloria	55–73
Hortus upsaliensis	172–210
Sponsalia plantarum	327–380
Curiositas naturalis	541–564

Vol. 2

Oeconomia naturæ	1–58
Pan Svecus	225–262
Oratio, qua peregrinationum intra patriam asseritor necessitas	408–429
Oratio de telluris incremento	430–472

Vol. 3

Plantæ hybridæ	28–62
Cui bono?	231–255
Vernatio arborum	363–376

Vol. 4

Metamorphosis plantarum	368–386
Calendarium floræ	387–414

Vol. 6

Generatio ambigena	1–16
Politia naturæ	17–39
Termini botanici	217–246
Fundamentum fructificationis	279–304

Vol. 10

Deliciæ naturæ	66–99
Disquisitio de sexu plantarum	100–131

Bref och skrifvelser af och till Carl von Linné med understöd af Svenska staten utgifna af Upsala universitet, utg. Th. M. Fries (afd. I, del 1–7) och J. M. Hulth (afd. I, del 7–8, afd. II, del 1). Stockholm och Upsala: Akademiska bokhandeln, 1907–1922.

Carl von Linnés ungdomsskrifter, saml. af Ewald Ährling och efter hans död med statsunderstöd utgifna af K. Vetenskaps-akademien, 1–2 serier. Stockholm: P. A. Norstedt och Söner, 1888–1889.

The Critica Botanica of Linnæus, translated by Sir Arthur Hort, revised by M. L. Green, with an introduction by Sir Arthur Hill. London: Ray Society, 1938.

Flora lapponica, exhibens plantas per Lapponiam crescentes, secundum systema sexuale, collectas in itinere impensis Soc. Reg. Scient. Upsaliensis, anno 1732 instituto. Additis synonymis, et locis natalibus omnium, descriptionibus et figuris rariorum, viribus medicatis et oeconomicis plurimarum. Editio altera, aucta et emendata studio et cura Jacobi Edvardi Smith. Londini: impensis B. White et Filiorum. Typis J. Davis, 1792.

Flora svecica, exhibens plantas per regnum Sveciæ crescentes, systematice cum differentiis specierum, synonymis autorum, nominibus incolarum, solo locorum, usu oeconomorum, officinalibus pharmacopæorum. Editio secunda aucta et emendata. Stockholmiæ sumtu et literis Laurentii Salvii, 1755.

Fundamenta botanica quæ majorum operum prodromi instar theoriam scientiæ botanices per breves aphorismos tradunt. Amstelodami, apud Salomonem Schouten, 1736.

Genera plantarum eorumque characteres naturales secundum numerum, figuram, situm, et proportionem omnium fructificationis partium. Lugduni Batavorum apud Conradum Wishoff, 1737.

Genera plantarum eorumque characteres naturales, secundùm numerum, figuram, situm, et proportionem omnium fructificationis partium . . . . Editio secunda, nominibus plantarum gallicis locupletata. Parisiis, sumptibus Michælis Antonii David . . .1743.

Genera plantarum eorumque characteres naturales secundum numerum, figuram, situm, et proportionem omnium fructificationis partium. . . . Editio sexta ab auctore reformata et aucta. Holmiæ, impensis direct. Laurentii Salvii. 1764.

Öländska och Gotländska resa på Riksens höglovlige ständers befallning förrättad år 1741. Med anmärkningar uti ekonomien, naturalhistorien, antikviteter etc. med åtskillige figurer, red. av Carl-Otto von Sydow. Stockholm: Wahlström och Widstrand, 1962.

Philosophia botanica in qva explicantur fundamenta botanica cum definitionibus partium, exemplis terminorum, observationibus rariorum, adjectis figuris æneis. Stockholmiæ, apud Godofr. Kiesewetter, 1751.

Translation: *The elements of botany: containing the history of the science: with accurate definitions of all the terms of art, exemplified in eleven copper-plates; the theory of vegetables; the scientific arrangement of plants, and names used in botany; rules concerning the general history, virtues, and uses of plants.* Being a translation of the *Philosophia botanica,* and other treatises of the celebrated Linnæus. To which is added, an appendix, wherein are described some plants lately found in Norfolk and Suffolk, illustrated with three additional copper-plates, all taken from the life. By Hugh Rose . . . London: Printed for T. Cadell . . . and M. Hingeston . . . 1775.

Prælectiones in ordines naturales plantarum. E propio et Jo. Chr. Fabricii . . . Edidit Paulus Diet. Giseke . . . Accessit uberior Palmarum et Scitaminum expositio præter plurium novorum generum reductiones cum mappa geographico-genealogica affinitatum ordinum, et aliquot fructuum palmarum figuræ . . . Hamburgi, impensis Benj. Gottl. Hoffmanni. Typis G. F. Schniebes. 1792.

Skrifter af Carl von Linné utgifna av Kungl. Svenska Vetenskapsakademien.
  2. Valda smärre skrifter af allmänt naturvetenskapligt innehåll af Carl von Linné dels af honom författade på svenska språket dels öfversatta af några hans lärjungar och Th. M. Fries. Upsala: Almqvist & Wiksell. 1906.
  3. Classes plantarum opus denuo editum. Ibid. 1907.
  4. Valda smärre skrifter af botaniskt innehåll af Carl von Linné dels af honom författade på svenska språket dels öfversatta af några hans lärjungar och Th. M. Fries. Ibid. 1908.

Skånska resa på höga överhetens befallning förrättad år 1749. Med rön och anmärkningar uti ekonomien, naturalier, antikviteter, seder, levnadssätt med tillhörige figurer, red. av Carl-Otto von Sydow. Stockholm: Wahlström och Widstrand, 1959.

Species plantarum. A Facsimile of the first edition, 1753, with an introduction by William T. Stearn. 2 vols. London: Ray Society, 1957–1959.

Systema Naturæ, sive regna tria naturæ systematice proposita per classes, ordines, genera, & species. Lugduni Batavorum, apud Theodorum Haak, 1735. Ex typographia Joannis Wilhelmi de Groot.

Systema naturæ per regna tria naturæ, secundum classes, ordines, genera, species, cum characteribus, differentiis, synonymis, locis. Editio decima tertia, aucta, reformata. Cura Jo. Frid. Gmelin . . . T. 1: P. 1–7; T. 2: P. 1–2; T. 3. Lipsiæ, 1788–1793. Impensis Georg. Emanuel. Beer.

Vita Caroli Linnæi, Carl von Linnés självbiografier, på uppdrag av Uppsala universitet utgivna af Elis Malmeström och Arvid Hj. Uggla. Stockholm: Almqvist & Wiksell, 1957.

Wästgöta-resa, på Rikens Högloflige Ständers befallning förrättad år 1746. Med anmärkningar uti oeconomien, naturkunnogheten, antiquiteter, inwånarnes seder och lefnads-sätt, med tilhörige figurer . . . Nytryck efter originalupplagan 1747 med textkommentar av Natanael Beckman. Göteborg: Thulin och Ohlson antikvarisk bokhandel, 1928.

II.   Primary Sources Other Than The Works of Carl von Linné

Adanson, Michel. "Préface Istorike sur l'état ancien et actuel de la Botanike, et une Téorie de cette science." In *Familles des Plantes,* Ire Partie, pp. i–cccxxv. Paris: Vincent, 1763.

Aristotle, *Categories and De Interpretatione,* translated by J. L. Ackrill. Oxford: Clarendon, 1963.

————. *Selections,* edited by W. D. Ross. New York: Scribners, 1927.

————. *The Works of Aristotle,* translated into English under the editorship of W. D. Ross. Oxford: Clarendon.

The following works have been cited:

Volume I, *Analytica Priora,* translated by A. J. Jenkinson, and *Analytica Posteriora,* translated by G. R. G. Mure, 1928.

Volume IV, *Historia Animalium,* translated by D'Arcy Wentworth Thompson, 1910.

Volume V, *De Partibus Animalium,* translated by William Ogle, 1912.

Volume VIII, *Metaphysica,* translated by W. D. Ross, 1928.

Bauhin, Gaspard, [*Phytopinax*] φυτοπιναξ: *seu, Envmeratio plantarvm ab herbariis nostro seculo descriptarum cum earum differentiis: cvi plurimarum hactenus ab iisdem non descriptarum succinctae descriptiones & denominationes accesêre: additis aliquot hactenus non sculptarum plantarvm viuis iconibus:* . . . Basileæ: per Sebastianvm Henricpetri, 1596.

————. [*Prodromos*] πρόδρομοs *theatri botanici in qvo plantæ svpra sexcentæ ab ipso primum descriptæ cum plurimis figuris proponuntur.* Ed. 2 emendatior. Basileæ: impensis Joannis regis, 1671.

————. [*Pinax*] πίναξ *Theatri botanici sive Index in Theophrasti, Dioscorides, Plinii et botanicorvm qui à seculo scripserunt opera plantarum circiter sex millivm ab ipsis exhibitarvm nomina cum earundem synonymijs et differentijs methodice secundum genera & species proponens.* Opvs XL. annorvm summopere expetitum ad autoris autographum recensitum. Basileæ: impensis Joannis regis, 1671.

Bock, Hieronymus. *Kreüter Bůch. Darinn unterscheidt Namen vnnd Würckung der Kreütter, Stauden, Hecken vnd Beümen, sampt jren Früchten, so inn Teütschen Landen wachsen, auch der selbigen eigentlicher vnnd wolgegründter gebrauch in der Artznei, fleissig dargeben, Leibs gesundheit zů fürden vnnd zu behalten sehr nutzlich vnd tröstlich, vorab dem gemeinen einfaltigen Man* . . . auss langwiriger und gewisser erfarung beschriben. . . . Mit keiserlicher Freiheit auff Achtjar. Gedruckt zu Strassburg, im Jar M.D.LX.

Brunfels, Otto. *Herbarvm vivæ eicones, ad naturę imitationen, suma cum diligentia et artificio effigiatæ, unà cum effectibus earundem, in gratiam ueteris illius et iamiam renascentis herbariae medicinæ* . . . recens editæ M.D.XXX. Quibus adiecta ad calcem, appendix isagogica de usu & administratione simplicivm. Item index contentorū singulorum. Argentorati apud I. Schottū cum Cæs. Majest. privilegio ad sexennium.

Buffon, Georges Louis de. *Histoire naturelle générale et particulière, avec la description du Cabinet du Roi.* 15 vols. Paris: Imprimerie Royale, 1749–1767.

Cæsalpino [Andreas Cæsalpinus]. *De Plantis libri XVI.* Florence: Marescot, 1583.

————. *Questionum Peripateticorum Libri quinque.* Juntas, 1571.

Partial Translation: Césalpin, *Questions Péripatéticiennes*, traduction de Maurice Dorolle. Paris: Librairie Félix Alcan, 1929.

Candolle, Augustin-Pyrame de. *Essai sur les propriétés médicales des Plantes, comparées avec leurs formes extérieures et leur classification naturelle.* Paris: Didot Jeune, 1804.

————. *Théorie élémentaire de la Botanique, ou Exposition des principes de la classification naturelle et de l'Art de décrire et d'étudier les végétaux,* 3ᵉ édition. Paris: Librairie Encyclopédique de Roret, 1844.

Cordus, Valerius, *Annotationes in Pedacij Dioscoridis Anazarbei De Medica materia libros V. Longè aliæ quam ante hac sunt euulgatæ. Eijvsdem Val. Cordi Historiæ Stirpium Lib. IIII Posthumi, nunc primùm in lucem editi, adiectis etiam Stirpium iconibus: & breuissimus Annotatiunculus. Etc.* Omnia summo studio atque industria doctiss. atque excellentis viri Conr. Gesneri medici Tigurini collecta & præfationibus illustrata. Cum Gratia & Privilegio Cæsaro ad annos oct. M.D.XLI.

Dodoens, Rembert. *Stirpium historiæ pemptades sex sive libri XXX.* Antverpiæ: ex officina Christophori Plantini, 1583.

Fuchs, Leonhart. *De Historia stirpium commentarii insignes, maximis impensis & Vigiliis elaborati, . . .* Scholiis in singula propè capita longè utilissimis à viro quodam medicinæ doctissimo adiectis, & Plantarum voces Gallicas passim experimentibus. Accessitiis succincta admodum vocum difficilium & obscurarum passim in hoc opere occurentium explicatio. Unà cum triplici Indice, quorum primus quidem Stirpium nomenclaturas Græcas, alter Latinas, tertius officinis Seplasiarorū & herbariis vsitatis, continet. Parisiis. Apud Audoenum Paruum sub Lilio Aureo, via ad diuum Iacobum. 1546.

Jussieu, Antoine-Laurent de. *Genera Plantarum secundum ordines naturales disposita, juxta methodum in horto regio parisiensi exaratam anno MDCCLXXIV.* Paris: Hérissant, 1789.

————. *Principes de la Méthode Naturelle des Végétaux, Article extrait du 30ᵉ Vol., Dictionnaire des sciences naturelles.* Paris: F. G. Levrault, 1824.

Jussieu, Bernard de. "Histoire d'une Plante connue par les Botanistes sous le nom de Pilularia." In *Mémoires de l'Academie des Sciences,* 1739, pp. 240–256.

Kant, Immanuel. "Erste Einleitung in die Kritik der Urteilskraft." In *Immanuel Kants Werke,* Band 5, herausgegeben von Ernst Cassirer, pp. 177–231, 581–605. Berlin: Bruno Cassirer, 1914.

Lamarck, Jean-Baptiste de Monet de, et Candolle, Augustin-Pyrame de. *Flore Françoise, ou Descriptions succinctes de toutes les Plantes qui croissent naturellement en France, etc. . . . . précédées par un Exposé des Principes élémentaires de la Botanique,* 3ᵉ édition, 6 vols. Paris: Desray, 1815.

l'Ecluse, Charles de. *Rariorvm Plantarum Historiæ.* Quæ accesserint, proxima pagina docebit. Antverpiæ: ex officina Plantiniana Apud Ioannem Moretum, 1601.

Leibniz, G. W. *Hauptschriften zur Grundlegung der Philosophie*, II. Band, herausgegeben von Artur Buchenau und Ernst Cassirer. Leipzig: Meiner, 1906.

l'Obel, Matthias, and Pena, Pierre. *Nova Stirpium Adversaria Perfacilis Vestigatio, luculentaqve accessio ad Priscorum, præsertim Dioscoridis, & Recentiorum, Materiam Medicam. . . . Quibus accessit Appendix cum Indice variarum linguarum locupletissimo. Eodem M. de Lobel Avctore. Additis Gvillielmi Rondelletii aliquot Remediorum formulis, nunquam antehac in lucem editis. Antverpiæ: Apud Christophorum Plantinum Architypographii Regum, MCLXXVI.*

Pulteney, Richard. *Historical and Biographical Sketches of the Progress of Botany in England from its Origin to the Introduction of the Linnæan System.* London: Cadell, 1790.

Ray, John. *The Correspondence of John Ray*, edited by Edwin Lankester. London: Ray Society, MDCCCXLVIII.

————. *Further Correspondence of John Ray*, edited by Robert W. T. Gunther. London: Ray Society, MCMXXVIII.

————. *Historia Plantarum Species hactenas editas aliasque insuper multas noviter inventas & descriptas complectens, in qua agitur primò De Plantis in Genere, Earumque Partibus, Accidentibus & Differentiis, Deinde Genera omnia tum summa tum subalterna ad Species usque infimas, Notis suis certis & Characteristicis Definita, Methodo Naturæ vestigiis insistente disponuntur; Species singulæ accurate describuntur, obscura illustrantur, omissa supplentur, superflua resecantur, Synonyma necessaria adjiciuntur; Vires denique & usus recepti compendio traduntur. . . .* Londini: Smith & Walford, 1686.

————. *Methodus Plantarum Nova, brevitatis & perspicuitatis causa synoptice in tabulis exhibita, cum notis generum tum summorum tum subalternorum characteristicis, observationibus nonnullis de seminibus plantarum & indice copioso . . . .* London: Faithorne & Kersey, 1682.

————. *Synopsis methodica stirpium britannicarum . . .* Ed. 2 Accessit Aug. Rivini epistola ad Joan Raium de methodo: cum ejusdem responsoria. London, 1691.

Royen, Adrian van. *Floræ Leydensis prodromus, exhibens plantas quæ in Horto academico lugduno-batavo aluntur.* Leyden: Luchtman, 1740.

Siegesbeck, Johann G. *Epicrisis in clarissimi Linnæi systema Plantarum sexuale in adjecta Botanosofiæ verioris brevi sciagrafia.* Petropoli: Typis Academiæ, 1734.

————. *Vaniloquentiæ Botanicæ specimen, a D. Gleditsch in Consideratione Epicrisios Sigesbekianæ in scripta Botanica Linnæi, pro rite obtinendo sexualistæ titulo nuper evulgatum, jure vero retorsionis refutatum et elusum.* Petropoli: Typis Academiæ, 1741.

Smith, James Edward. *A Selection of the Correspondence of Linnæus and other naturalists from the original manuscripts.* 2 vols. London: Longman, Hurst, Rees, Orme, and Brown, 1821.

Tournefort, Josef Pitton de. *Elemens de Botanique ou Methode pour connoître les Plantes.* 2 vols. Paris: Imprimerie Royale, 1694.

————. *Institutiones Rei Herbariæ*, Editio 3, appendicibus aucta ab Antonio de Jussieu. Parisiis: e Typographia Regia, 1719.

Partial Translation: "Isagoge in Rem Herbariam." In *Institutiones Rei Herbariæ*, I, traduit par G. Becker. *Tournefort*, collection dirigée par Roger Heim, préface par Roger Heim, pp. 241–306. Paris: Muséum National d'Histoire Naturelle, 1957.

————. *Relation d'un Voyage du Levant.* 3 vols. Lyon: Freres Bruyset, 1727.

Uggla, Arvid Hjalmar, "Linné den yngres brev till Abraham Bäck 1778." In *Svenska Linné-Sällskapets Årsskrift*, Årg. XXXIX–XL, 1956–57, pp. 138–165. Uppsala: Almqvist & Wiksell, 1957.

————. "Linné den yngres brev till Abraham Bäck. 2. 1779–1783." In *Svenska Linné-Sällskapets Årsskrift*, Årg. XLI, pp. 61–100. 1959.

III.   Secondary Sources

Arber, Agnes. *Herbals. Their Origin and Evolution. A Chapter in the History of Botany, 1470–1670.* Cambridge: Cambridge University Press, 1912.

————. *The Natural Philosophy of Plant Form.* Cambridge: Cambridge University Press, 1950.

Balme, D. M. "ΓΕΝΟΣ and ΕΙΔΟΣ in Aristotle's Biology." *Classical Quarterly* 12 (1): 81–98.

Bremekamp, C. E. B. "Linné's Significance for the Development of Phytography." *Taxon* 2 (3): 47–54.

————. "Linné's Views on the Hierarchy of the Taxonomic Groups." *Acta Botanica Neerlandica* 2 (2): 242–253.

————. "A Re-examination of Cæsalpino's Classification." *Acta Botanica Neerlandica* 1 (4): 580–593.

Burckhardt, Rud. "J.-V. Carus, Geschichte der Zoologie, 1872." *Zoologische Annalen* 1 (1905): 355–375.

Cain, A. J. "Function and Taxonomic Importance." *Systematics Association Publication Number 3* (November 1959): 5–19.

————. "Logic and Memory in Linnæus's System of Taxonomy," *Proceedings of the Linnæan Society of London* 169 (1 and 1): 144–163.

Cassirer, Ernst. *Das Erkenntnisproblem in der Philosophie und Wissenschaft der neueren Zeit*, I. Band. Berlin: Cassirer, 1911.

————. *The Problem of Knowledge. Philosophy, Science, and History since Hegel.* Translated by William H. Woglom and Charles W. Hendel, with a preface by Charles W. Hendel. New Haven: Yale University Press, 1950.

————. *Substanzbegriff und Funktionsbegriff.* Berlin: Cassirer, 1910.

Choate, Helen A. "The Origin and Development of the Binomial System of Nomenclature." *The Plant World* 15 (1912): 257–263.

Couturat, Louis. *La Logique de Leibniz.* Paris: Librairie Félix Alcan, 1901.

Cuénot, L. *L'Espèce.* Paris: Doin & Cie, 1936.

Daudin, Henri. *Cuvier et Lamarck, les Classes Zoologiques et l'idée de série animale (1790–1830).* 2 vols. Paris: Librairie Félix Alcan, 1926.

————. *De Linné à Jussieu, Méthodes de la Classification et idée de série en botanique et en zoologie (1740–1790).* Paris: Librairie Félix Alcan, 1926.

Drobisch, Moritz W. *Neue Darstellung der Logik.* Hamburg & Leipzig: Voss, 1887.

Dughi, R. "Tournefort dans l'histoire de la botanique." In *Tournefort*, collection dirigée par Roger Heim, préface par Roger Heim, pp. 131–185. Paris: Muséum National d'Histoire Naturelle, 1957.

Gertz, Otto. "Linnés blomsterrabatter å Hammarby på Linnés tid." *Svenska Linné-Sällskapets Årsskrift.* Årg. X, 1927, pp. 30–56. Uppsala: Almqvist & Wiksell, 1927.

Hamelin, O., *Le Système d'Aristote.* Paris: Librairie Félix Alcan, 1920.

Heller, John Lewis. "Index auctorum et librorum a Linnæo (*Species Plantarum*, 1753) citatorum." *Species Plantarum*, a Facsimile of the first edition, 1753. Vol. 2, pp. 3–60. London: Ray Society, 1959.

Hering, Jean. "Bemerkungen über das Wesen, die Wesenheit und die

Idee." *Jahrbuch für Philosophie und phänomenologische Forschung,* pp. 495–543. Halle: Max Niemeyer, 1921.

Hofsten, Nils von. "Linnés naturuppfattning." *Svenska Linné-Sällskapets Årsskrift.* Årg. XLI, 1958, pp. 13–35. Uppsala: Almqvist & Wiksell, 1959.

————. "Skapelsetro och uralstringshypoteser före Darwin." *Uppsala universitets årsskrift 1928,* program 2, pp. 3–73. Uppsala: Almqvist & Wiksell, 1928.

————. "Systema naturæ, ett tvåhundraårsminne," *Svenska Linné-Sällskapets Årsskrift.* Årg. XVIII, pp. 1–15. Uppsala: Almqvist & Wiksell, 1935.

Hull, David L. "The Effect of Essentialism on Taxonomy. Two Thousand Years of Stasis, I & II." *The British Journal for the Philosophy of Science* 15, 16 (60 and 61): 314–326, 1–18.

Hulth, J. M. *Bibliographia Linnæana, Matériaux pour servir à une bibliographie Linnéenne.* Partie I, livraison I. Uppsala, Berlin: Librairie de l'Université et R. Friedländer & Sohn, 1907.

Jackson, Benjamin Daydon. "Index to the Linnæan Herbarium, with indications of the types of species marked by Carl von Linné." Forming a supplement to *Proceedings of the Linnæan Society of London* 124: 7–152.

Kapp, Ernst. *Greek Foundations of Traditional Logic.* New York: Columbia, 1942.

Leroy, J. F. "Tournefort et la classification végétal." In *Tournefort,* collection dirigée par Roger Heim, préface par Roger Heim, pp. 187–206. Paris: Muséum National d'Histoire Naturelle, 1957.

Lindman, C. A. M. "Carl von Linné såsom botanist." In *Carl von Linnés betydelse såsom naturforskare och läkare.* Uppsala: Almqvist & Wiksell, 1907.

Linnell, Tore. "Några ord om Linnés Peloria och dess locus classicus." In *Svenska Linné-Sällskapets Årsskrift,* Årg. XXXV, 1952, pp. 62–70. Uppsala: Almqvist & Wiksell, 1953.

Lovejoy, Arthur O. *The Great Chain of Being, A Study of the History of an Idea.* Cambridge, Massachusetts: Harvard University Press, 1936.

Malmeström, Elis, *Carl von Linnés religiösa åskådning,* Akademisk avhandling. Stockholm: Svenska kyrkans diakonistyrelsens bokförlag, 1926.

Mayr, Ernst. "Agassiz, Darwin, and Evolution." *Harvard Library Bulletin* 13 (2): 165–194.

————. *Animal Species and Evolution.* Cambridge, Massachusetts: Belknap Press, 1963.

————. "The Evolutionary Significance of the Systematic Categories." *Systematics of to-day,* . . . Edited by Olov Hedberg, *Uppsala universitets årsskrift 1958:6,* pp. 13–20. Uppsala: A.-B. Lundequistska bokhandel, 1958.

————. "Illiger and the Biological Species Concept." *Journal of the History of Biology* 1 (2): 163–178.

————. *Systematics and the Origin of Species.* New York: Columbia, 1942.

————. "Theory of Biological Classification." *Nature* 220 (5167): 545–548.

Mayr, Ernst, ed. "Species Concepts and Definitions." *The Species Problem. A Symposium.* American Association for the Advancement of Science, no. 50, pp. 1–22. Washington, D.C., 1957.

Metzger, Hélène. *Les Concepts Scientifiques.* Paris: Librairie Félix Alcan, 1926.

Meyer, Ernst H. F. *Geschichte der Botanik.* Königsberg: Bornträger, 1856.

Meyer, Jürgen Bona. *Aristoteles Thierkunde. Ein Beitrag zur Geschichte der Zoologie, Physiologie und alten Philosophie.* Berlin: Reimer, 1855.

Nannfeldt, J. A. "Presidential Address." In *Systematics of to-day,* . . . Edited by Olov Hedberg, *Uppsala universitets årsskrift 1958:6,* pp. 7–12. Uppsala: A.-B. Lundequistska bokhandel, 1958.

————. "Species Plantarum. Ett 200-årsminne." *Svenska Linné-Sällskapets Årsskrift,* Årg. XXXVI, 1953, pp. 1–9. Uppsala: Almqvist & Wiksell, 1954.

Pennell, F. W. "Genotypes of the Scrophulariaceæ in the first edition of the 'Species Plantarum'." *Proceedings of the Academy of Natural Science, Philadelphia* 82: 9–26.

Piaget, Jean. "La Pensée Biologique." *Introduction à l'Épistémologie Génétique.* Vol. 3, pp. 5–128. Paris: P.U.F., 1950.

Popper, Karl R. *The Open Society and Its Enemies.* Princeton: Princeton University Press, 1950.

Prantl, Carl. *Geschichte der Logik im Abendlande,* I. Band. Leipzig: Hirzel, 1855.

Rádl, Em. *Geschichte der Biologischen Theorien seit dem Ende des siebzehnten Jahrhunderts,* I. Teil. Leipzig: Engelmann, 1905.

Randall, John Herman, Jr. *The Career of Philosophy*. Vol. 1. New York: Columbia, 1962.

————. "The Development of Scientific Method in the School of Padua." *Journal of the History of Ideas* 1 (1940): 177–206.

Raven, Charles E. *John Ray, Naturalist, His Life and Works*. Cambridge: Cambridge University Press, 1942.

Runes, Dagobert D. *The Classics in Logic*. New York: Philosophical Library, 1962.

Sachs, Julius von. *History of Botany (1530–1860)*. Translated by H. E. F. Garnsey, revised by Isaac Bayley Balfour. Oxford: Clarendon, 1890.

Savage, Spencer. *A catalogue of the Linnæan herbarium*. Compiled and annotated by Spencer Savage. London: Linnæan Society, 1945.

Soulsby, B. H. *A catalogue of the works of Linnæus (and publications more immediately relating thereto) preserved in the Libraries of the British Museum*, 2nd ed. London: Trustees of the British Museum, 1933.

Sprague, T. A., "The Plan of the Species Plantarum." *Proceedings of the Linnæan Society of London* 165 (2): 151–156.

Stearn, William T. "An Introduction to the *Species Plantarum* and cognate botanical works of Carl Linnæus." In *Species Plantarum*, A Facsimile of the first edition, 1753, vol. 1, pp. 1–176. London: Ray Society, 1957.

————. *Three Prefaces on Linnæus and Robert Brown*. Weinheim: J. Cramer, 1962.

Svenson, H. K., "On the Descriptive Method of Linnæus." *Rhodora* 47 (562 and 563): 273–302, 363–388.

Thienemann, August. *Die Stufenfolge der Dinge, der Versuch eines natürlichen Systems der Naturkörper aus dem achtzehnten Jahrhundert. Zoologische Annalen* 3 (1910): 185–274.

Uggla, Arvid Hjalmar. "Linné och Linnéanerna." *Ny illustrerad svensk litteraturhistoria*, 2. delen. Stockholm: Natur och Kultur, 1956.

————. "Om förhistorien till Species Plantarum." *Svenska Linné-Sällskapets Årsskrift*, Årg. XXXVI, pp. 10–16. Uppsala: Almqvist & Wiksell, 1954.

Vines, Sydney Howard. "Robert Morison and John Ray." In *Makers of British Botany*. Edited by F. W. Oliver. Cambridge: Cambridge University Press, 1913.

Zimmermann, Walter. *Evolution, die Geschichte ihrer Probleme und Erkenntnisse*. München: Freiburg, 1953.

Index

PRINCIPAL WORKS BY LINNÉ

Index

PROPER NAMES

Index